The Crime Scene Photographer

Other titles in Lucent's Crime Scene Investigations series include:

The Crime Scene Photographer

by Gail B. Stewart

LUCENT BOOKS
A part of Gale, Cengage Learning

GALE
CENGAGE Learning™

Detroit • New York • San Francisco • New Haven, Conn • Waterville, Maine • London

© 2008 Gale, Cengage Learning

ALL RIGHTS RESERVED. No part of this work covered by the copyright herein may be reproduced, transmitted, stored, or used in any form or by any means graphic, electronic, or mechanical, including but not limited to photocopying, recording, scanning, digitizing, taping, Web distribution, information networks, or information storage and retrieval systems, except as permitted under Section 107 or 108 of the 1976 United States Copyright Act, without the prior written permission of the publisher.

Every effort has been made to trace the owners of copyrighted material.

LIBRARY OF CONGRESS CATALOGING-IN-PUBLICATION DATA

Stewart, Gail B. (Gail Barbara), 1949–
   The crime scene photographer / by Gail B. Stewart.
      p. cm. — (Crime scene investigations)
   Includes bibliographical references and index.
   ISBN 978-1-4205-0036-3 (hardcover)
   1. Legal photography—United States—Juvenile literature. I. Title.
   HV6071.S73 2008
   363.25'2—dc22

                                                            2008018285

Lucent Books
27500 Drake Rd.
Farmington Hills, MI 48331

ISBN-13: 978-1-4205-0036-3
ISBN-10: 1-4205-0036-8

Printed in the United States of America
2 3 4 5 6 7 12 11 10 09 08

Contents

Foreword

The popularity of crime scene and investigative crime shows on television has come as a surprise to many who work in the field. The main surprise is the concept that crime scene analysts are the true crime solvers, when in truth, it takes dozens of people, doing many different jobs, to solve a crime. Often, the crime scene analyst's contribution is a small one. One Minnesota forensic scientist says that the public "has gotten the wrong idea. Because I work in a lab similar to the ones on *CSI*, people seem to think I'm solving crimes left and right—just me and my microscope. They don't believe me when I tell them that it's the investigators that are solving crimes, not me."

Crime scene analysts do have an important role to play, however. Science has rapidly added a whole new dimension to gathering and assessing evidence. Modern crime labs can match a hair of a murder suspect to one found on a murder victim, for example, or recover a latent fingerprint from a threatening letter, or use a powerful microscope to match tool marks made during the wiring of an explosive device to a tool in a suspect's possession.

Probably the most exciting of the forensic scientist's tools is DNA analysis. DNA can be found in just one drop of blood, a dribble of saliva on a toothbrush, or even the residue from a fingerprint. Some DNA analysis techniques enable scientists to tell with certainty, for example, whether a drop of blood on a suspect's shirt is that of a murder victim.

While these exciting techniques are now an essential part of many investigations, they cannot solve crimes alone. "DNA doesn't come with a name and address on it," says the Minnesota forensic scientist. "It's great if you have someone in custody to match the sample to, but otherwise, it doesn't help. That's the investigator's job. We can have all the great DNA evidence in the world, and without a suspect, it will just sit on the shelf. We've all seen cases with very little forensic evidence get solved by the resourcefulness of a detective."

While forensic specialists get the most media attention today, the work of detectives still forms the core of most criminal investigations. Their job, in many ways, has changed little over the years. Most cases are still solved through the persistence and determination of a criminal detective whose work may be anything but glamorous. Many cases require routine, even mind-numbing tasks. After the July 2005 bombings in London, for example, police officers sat in front of video players watching thousands of hours of closed-circuit television tape from security cameras throughout the city, and as a result were able to get the first images of the bombers.

The Lucent Books Crime Scene Investigations series explores the variety of ways crimes are solved. Titles cover particular crimes such as murder, specific cases such as the killing of three civil rights workers in Mississippi, or the role specialists such as medical examiners play in solving crimes. Each title in the series demonstrates the ways a crime may be solved, from the various applications of forensic science and technology to the reasoning of investigators. Sidebars examine both the limits and possibilities of the new technologies and present crime statistics, career information, and step-by-step explanations of scientific and legal processes.

The Crime Scene Investigations series strives to be both informative and realistic about how members of law enforcement —criminal investigators, forensic scientists, and others—solve crimes, for it is essential that student researchers understand that crime solving is rarely quick or easy. Many factors—from a detective's dogged pursuit of one tenuous lead to a suspect's careless mistakes to sheer luck to complex calculations computed in the lab—are all part of crime solving today.

A Thousand Heartbreaking Words

The pictures are in no particular order. Each tells a story, or at least part of one. In one a basement window has been broken. A few shards of glass are still clinging to the frame, but the space is large enough for someone to have climbed through. A large footprint—perhaps that of a man wearing a work boot—is visible in the mud next to the window.

Some of the pictures are even more graphic. One shows part of a human skeleton—a skull and several bones. There are bits of clothing hanging on some of the bones, which are partially covered in dirt. Another picture shows a man lying facedown in the street. Pools of blood are next to his head and near his stomach. The last photo is a close-up of a woman's hand. The hand looks distorted, and it is clear that two of the fingers are broken. There is what looks like blood and bits of something else under her fingernails.

The last picture is that of a little boy, perhaps two years old. He is standing, facing the camera. His eyes seem blank, as if he were looking at something only he can see. He is shirtless, and his stomach and chest are covered with bruises. Some appear to be fresh; others look as though they have been there longer.

From Temporary to Permanent

These photographs are all aspects of crime scenes. They were taken by photographers working with city, county, or state police departments throughout the United States. Each of them is a necessary part of a crime investigation.

The photographer at the scene of a crime is not the detective. He or she is not the one who will make an arrest or interrogate suspects. But the photographer has the great responsibility of documenting the crime scene. By taking pictures of every detail of the scene, the photographer can preserve it. If the job is done well, an investigating detective can view the photographs and be able to see every aspect of the crime scene. From the position of the body at a homicide to the details of

The crime scene photographer is crucial for a thorough criminal investigation.

fingerprints on a kitchen counter, the scene will be accurately documented.

Amy, a forensic technician, says:

Police hold up a sheet to shield the body of an infant while the crime scene photographer creates a permanent visual record of the discovery.

That's really, really vital. In my opinion, nobody at the crime scene has a more important job. By nature, crime scenes are temporary. Take a homicide. Once the body is taken away and the blood and whatever is cleaned up, and the yellow crime scene tape comes down, the scene isn't there anymore. Things are moved around, cleaned up, whatever. And whatever that scene could tell investigators won't be there anymore. So the pho-

tographer is the one who turns a temporary scene into a permanent record.[1]

Creating permanence from a temporary crime scene is especially important when investigators are unable to solve a case quickly. Sometimes detectives may lack an important witness or a piece of evidence that would let them charge a suspect. Months or even years later, evidence or a witness may be found. And the photographs taken at the scene can enable investigators to revisit it.

A Nagging Feeling That Something Looked Wrong

Sometimes, too, what was really a murder may have been originally viewed as an accident. In some cases, it is a photograph from the original scene that establishes the truth. That happened in western Michigan in 2000, when a four-year-old girl was killed by a shotgun blast. Her mother told investigators that the girl had been playing with a vacuum cleaner that had a small attachment for getting in corners. There was a shotgun lying on the bed, the mother said. The girl poked the trigger with the vacuum attachment and the gun fired, killing her.

Though the detectives at the scene wrote the death off as accidental, one of them began having doubts later. Something looked wrong in the photographs, but he could not say what it was. He approached a crime lab technician months after the incident and asked if they could take a look at the photos.

The crime lab people examined the photos and agreed with the detective that there was something troubling. One of them noticed that the gun was lying on the bed near the dead child. That was odd, remembers the lab director: "If the shotgun had discharged on the bed, you would have had huge burn patterns in the bed surface from the muzzle blast; the blankets would be all shredded; the gun would have recoiled backwards, been thrown off the bed. The pictures showed the gun lying on the bed still."[2]

The lab director, together with the detective, interviewed the mother, who finally confessed to shooting her daughter. The reason, she explained, was that her boyfriend had wanted them to move to Florida, but he did not want to take the girl. So the mother shot the little girl.

"These Stay With You"

By its very nature, crime scene photography is disturbing. Even the technicians and forensic experts who routinely take such photographs occasionally find themselves haunted by them. Forensic technician Steve Banning says that it is the child victims that are especially hard. "It bothers me, I see a child killed in a fire, for instance," he says. "And maybe she's wearing a pair of pajamas like one of my grandkids, or there's a toy at the scene that I've seen a hundred times at home. That really gets to me."[3]

The Minnesota technician who took the picture of the bruised toddler agrees. The technician explains:

Lots of these photos are bad. We see stuff most people shouldn't ever have to look at. . . . But most of the time, I can deal with it. It's my job. But the ones of kids, those are tough. This boy had been abused by his mother's boyfriend. Finally, the mother got brave enough to turn the guy in. This photograph is one of several we took to document the boy's injuries. I took the photos in 2004. So it's been awhile. But these stay with you.[4]

There is an old saying that a picture is worth a thousand words. "Maybe some are worth more," says technician Amy. "You have to find a positive side of what you're doing. Maybe the photo you take is one that will help find and convict a child abuser or a murderer. You never know for sure which pictures will be especially helpful. So you go with that. They're helpful, but no less heartbreaking."[5]

CHAPTER 1

A Vital Responsibility

The use of photography by law enforcement is almost as old as photography itself. When cameras were first invented in 1839, police used them to take pictures of people arrested for various crimes. The photos would later be used in what were called rogues' galleries, the ancestors of the modern mug shot books—collections of photos of criminals that crime witnesses view. Sometimes photos of wanted felons would also be made into posters to alert the public about the danger they posed.

The first use of photography at a crime scene was a horse and buggy accident. A man claimed that a large mud hole in the road forced him to veer off into a farmer's field. Police took a picture of the road, so that they had a record of it in case the farmer brought the case to court.

"That's What You Do"

Since those days, photography has become a necessary part of every serious crime scene. The photographer's job is to capture everything at the scene on film. And that, notes forensic technician Amy, is far more difficult than anyone could imagine:

> Sometimes I'll see one of the CSI shows on TV, you know, and we laugh about those crime scenes. I mean, there's a dead body, in a really clean living room. And two glasses on the coffee table. Just the glasses. In fact, the whole room is clean, every flat surface. No magazines or yesterday's newspaper, or dirty dishes. No dirty socks or kid's permission slips from school like everyone else's houses have.[6]

This rogues' gallery of wanted criminals dates from the nineteenth century, when police began to use photography as an important crime-solving tool.

EDWARD DINKLEMAN,
ALIAS EDDIE MILLER — HUNTER — BOWMAN,
PICKPOCKET,
SHOP LIFTER AND HOTEL THIEF.

WALTER SHERIDAN,
ALIAS RALSTON — KEENE,
BANK SNEAK, FORGER AND
COUNTERFEITER.

WILLIAM COLEMAN,
ALIAS BILLY COLEMAN,
BURGLAR AND BANK SNEAK.

IKE VAIL,
ALIAS OLD IKE,
CONFIDENCE.

JOHN LARNEY,
ALIAS MOLLIE MATCHES,
BANK SNEAK AND BURGLAR.

EDWARD RICE,
ALIAS BIG RICE,
CONFIDENCE AND HOTEL SNEAK.

Amy says that crime scenes are usually far more chaotic. "You walk in and you see fifty or a hundred things that may or may not be important. Dirty dishes in the sink, stuff in the wastebasket, beer or pop cans lying around, a pad of paper by the phone, whatever. Who knows? And you say to yourself, 'Just start.' And that's what you do."[7]

And because that film record will be the only permanent documentation of the chaos at the crime scene, it is absolutely necessary for it to be accurate and complete. At a homicide scene, for instance, immediately after the photographer is finished, investigators and other law enforcement personnel move the body. They pick things up and examine them. They remove weapons and other important things to test in the lab. The scene will never look the same once the photographer has done his or her work. As former New York homicide detective Vernon Geberth stresses, "Do it right the first time. You only get one chance."[8]

Who the Photographers Are

In most small towns throughout the United States, police officers themselves do much of the photography. Police departments often issue disposable cameras to their officers to document automobile accidents or assaults. In the case of a more serious crime such as homicide, they usually send for technicians from a nearby city. In larger cities, on the other hand, the photographers are part of the city's forensic crime lab. They are often organized into teams, or field units, that not only photograph the crime scene, but also process and collect fingerprints, blood samples, and other evidence. Once back in the crime lab, the members of the field units evaluate, examine, and test whatever they have gathered.

But whether the department is in a rural town in the Midwest or a large city, good crime scene photography requires a great deal of technical skill. Dencell, a former New York forensic technician, explains:

> It's not point and shoot. It's not the same as taking a picture at your daughter's birthday party. For instance, you take light. Crime scenes never seem to have enough light. You're always trying to make sure you have the right amount to get the details, say of a fingerprint. But you don't want too much, so that you overpower those details. You have

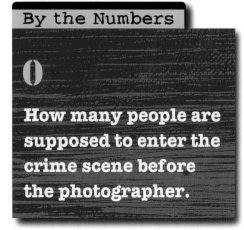

By the Numbers

0

How many people are supposed to enter the crime scene before the photographer.

Finding a Sense of Balance

"**I**'ve had murders of younger than three months to 83 years old," says forensic scientist Michael Calistro. "And everything in between. And I've seen just about everything in police work and in the military, so I've seen a lot. It doesn't usually bother me. I try to look at photography as a tool, a way of learning how the body works, how the heart and vessels work, that kind of thing. I don't want it to get to me, then I can't do my job. You look at it, you get angry. But with a very young victim, I just rationalize that the child is in heaven, and I'm speaking for the dead. They're gone. But I'm going to find out what happened. And I'll help get the information to assist the jury so it makes the right decision. That puts the job into perspective. Otherwise, you'd go nuts.

"This is a hard job, not a good job. All the excitement of being in law enforcement, of being involved in cases, it wears off after five years. It's like you get up in the morning and say, 'What am I going to see today?'"

Michael Calistro, personal interview, November 26, 2007, Minneapolis, MN.

to make sure you get enough light to really show the scene. You've got to get it right, so everything is visible, without shadows.[9]

Just as crucial as technical skill are a photographer's insight at the crime scene. To be a good crime scene photographer, it is important to be able to understand what detectives will find valuable even before they ask for it. "One thing I learned in the field is how much of a self-starter you have to be," Dencell says. "You can't sit around waiting for a detective to tell you what to do. You may start out needing direction, but eventually you need to figure out for yourself what detectives will need, and go from there."[10]

He believes that hands-on experience is the key. "The more scenes you do, the better you get, the more things you see," he says. "You aren't as distracted by the things that distract you when you first start, like the smells, the disorder of the room, the bodies—things like that. You just get better."[11]

Tough Training

One Minnesota detective says he started out, as all police officers in the state did years ago, as a crime scene photographer. He believes it was his class's final test that taught him an important fact about what crime scene photography really entails—and prepared him for what lay ahead.

During this crime scene mock-up used for criminal investigation training, investigators try to ascertain how many times a dummy was shot.

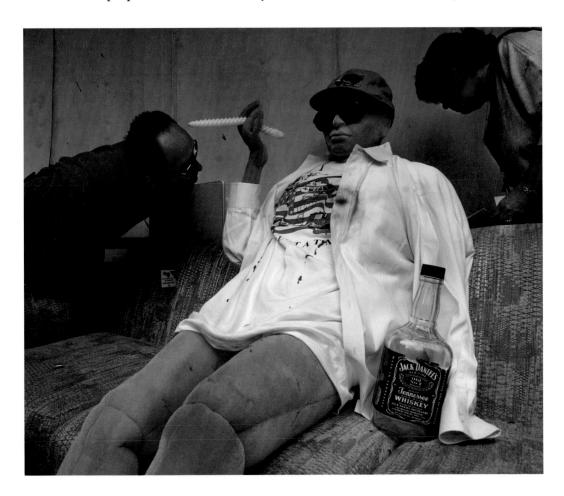

The instructor had taken the class to an unused area of the stockyards in south Saint Paul. The forensic staff had set up mock crime scenes in several different rooms, and the students had to photograph them all, without missing key details—frozen footprints in the mud, blood on the floor, and so on. It was January, the detective recalls, and it was bitter cold. And while his instructor sat comfortably in a heated van outside the stockyards, the students did their work. Says the detective: "We were out there, documenting these crime scenes, in these smelly old buildings—they just reeked of cow manure and blood and dead animals. And [the instructor] made us be out there all day long . . . and our cameras were freezing up while we were out there, because it was about ten below outside all day long."[12]

The detective says that the experience taught them all a very important lesson—one that had nothing to do with the mock crimes themselves. "I know now what they were trying to do with us that day," he says. "They were trying to get us used to what actual crime scenes are like. They're smelly. They're messy. And you're there for hours and hours, processing them."[13]

A Photograph's Value

One thing photographers know for certain is that even with the discomfort and difficulty of the job, their work can yield valuable results. As mentioned earlier, crime scene photographs can help refresh the memory of detectives about the position of key evidence. But they can occasionally make an even more dramatic contribution. Occasionally, a photograph can show information that discounts a suspect's story or prove that a key witness is lying. Minneapolis crime lab supervisor Bill Hinz gives an example:

We routinely do a series of photos panning the area around the body at an outside homicide. You're basically walking a circle with your back to the body and taking pictures of the whole area. That can come in handy. For instance, we've had times when we get a witness that says he saw the whole thing from his apartment, saw the homicide take place.

But it's happened, where we can look back on those photos and say, "No way, you can't even see that apartment from the crime scene. Hey, if we can't see your apartment window, we know you absolutely couldn't have seen the homicide happen." The photos don't prove the guy is guilty of murder. But it certainly does prove that he was lying about what he saw.[14]

By the Numbers

16,000

Number of forensic photographs taken at the site of the World Trade Center after September 11, 2001.

Something Wasn't Right

In some cases an inconsistency between a photo and the information given to detectives can determine whether a crime has been committed at all. In one 2002 case in northern Michigan, police received a frantic call from a woman. Her husband was dead of a gunshot wound, and although the gun lay close to his body, she was convinced he had been murdered. He had been involved with some very rough men, she told police, and they had threatened him several times.

The police officers had taken photos of the scene, but they viewed it as an obvious suicide. The man, they believed, had shot himself in the head—and evidence backed up that idea. There were powder burns on the man's temple. Powder burns result when a gun is fired very close to the skin. Also, fingerprints belonging to the victim were on the gun.

The man's wife was insistent. Her husband, she said, would never have committed suicide. It was not until days later, when she mentioned that her husband had been left-handed, that an alert detective took another look at the photographs. What they showed indicated that the woman's claims might be valid.

Becoming a Latent Fingerprint Analyst

Job Description:
The latent fingerprint analyst processes all evidence from a crime scene, looking for latent prints; recovers latent prints by using a wide array of chemicals; and photographs and makes copies of each print that is to be used as evidence in the investigation. The examiner is also responsible for entering minutiae, or tiny variant details, of fingerprints into the AFIS system so the print can be compared to fingerprints already on file.

Education:
Each city or county has its own requirements for employment, but most expect at least two years of college, with advanced certification showing the applicant has mastered the study of fingerprint analysis.

Qualifications:
One must have a complete knowledge of chemicals, powders, and forensic light sources used in processing and developing latent prints. Also, the applicant must be capable of photographing such prints.

Salary:
An entry-level latent fingerprint analyst usually earns a salary ranging from $42,000 to $58,000.

They realized that there was a good chance the man had not committed suicide after all.

The photos showed that the man had been shot in his right temple. That would not have been possible if he had used his left hand. It was very possible that someone had staged the suicide, not realizing that the man was left-handed. The inconsistency shown in those photographs was sufficient evidence for detectives to reopen the case and to begin investigating it as a homicide.

On Trial

Detectives rely on crime scene photographs as they work to solve a case. But the photographs can be equally important once the case goes to trial. Photographs of key aspects of a crime scene can allow juries to see evidence, rather than just hear about it secondhand from a detective or other witness.

"A lot of times, juries hear a medical examiner talking about the injuries sustained by the victim of a crime," says Dave, a retired police officer who has testified in many

As part of the evidence in a murder trial, the prosecuting attorney shows the jury an enlarged photo of the victim and the surrounding crime scene.

court cases. "And it is completely accurate, but the scientific terminology—even when they try to dumb it down for the rest of us—doesn't really show the real effects of those injuries."[15]

Bill Hinz agrees. He once took photographs of the injuries inflicted upon a woman by her ex-boyfriend. After abducting her, the man had used a lighter to heat the tip of a fingernail file, and used that object to cause a terrific burn in her vaginal area. "The photo showed the detail of that burn—you could even see the tiny hash mark pattern on the skin from that file," he says. "That photo showed exactly how horrific the burn was in ways that no words could really do. And as a result, the jury convicted the guy."[16]

Life? Or Death?

Sometimes the viewing of photographs by a jury is a key element in how a criminal is sentenced. In fact, it may make the difference between life and death. In July 2001 Massachusetts teenager Jonathan Rizzo was murdered. A forty-four-year-old man named Gary Sampson confessed to Rizzo's murder and that of two other men. During the trial concerning Rizzo's murder, Sampson said that he had been hitchhiking, and Rizzo stopped to give him a ride. Sampson forced Rizzo to stop the car and forced him into nearby woods, where he tied Rizzo to a tree. After promising Rizzo that he would not harm him, Sampson slit his throat and stabbed him numerous times.

Because Sampson had confessed to Rizzo's murder, he did not get a jury trial. However, prosecutors wanted him to receive the death penalty. For sentencing in this case, a jury in a U.S. District Court had to find that the death penalty was warranted in this crime. The jury would be in charge of determining that.

Prosecutors believed the crime scene photographs would allow the jury to see that the killing was especially cruel—something that the prosecution would have to demonstrate before someone could be sentenced to death in the United States. The judge then asked the jury to view photographs. First, however, he had Rizzo's family leave the courtroom, so their reaction would not sway the jury.

"This Was the Hardest Thing I've Ever Done in My Life"

In the crime scene photographs, writes a court reporter, the victim was "tied at the wrists, his arms pulled behind him and around a tree." He was "facedown on the forest floor, stabbed numerous times in the torso. A bandana had been tied around his head to cover his mouth. His shirt, which had his name tag [from the restaurant where he had worked] on it, was soaked with blood."[17]

Members of the jury were visibly shaken by the photographs. Two of them cried as the photos were shown. And Rizzo's family, in their special room, also had the opportunity to view the photographs—though some did not want to. Michael Rizzo, the victim's father, said that even though it had been more than two years since his son's death, the experience of seeing the actual crime scene was devastating. "It was awful," his said afterward. "Next to telling my wife that our son was dead, this was the hardest thing I've ever done in my life."[18]

The photographs had the effect the prosecution hoped for. Sampson was sentenced to die by lethal injection.

"Here's the Kind of Mom She Was"

Sometimes, out of the hundreds of photographs taken at the scene, it is not the bloodiest or most gruesome photograph that has the most impact on the jury. One detective tells about a particularly violent case in which a young mother was strangled and raped. Her eight-year-old daughter was raped, too. The man who did it had been invited into their home—one of several acquaintances who were coming to watch a playoff

Convicted murderer Gary Sampson is escorted by officers after he is sentenced to death. The jury gave Sampson the death penalty verdict after viewing horrific photographic evidence of the crime scene.

By the Numbers

1/1,000th

The fraction of a second that is the fastest shutter speed on a crime scene camera.

basketball game on television. For various reasons, the detective explained to the jury, at the last minute the other people invited could not attend—leaving the woman and her daughter alone with the man.

The detective recalls that the defense attorney tried to make it seem as though the crime were partly the fault of the mother. The attorney wanted to show that she was a bad mother and her bad judgment was in part responsible for the crimes against her and her daughter. That way his client might get a lighter sentence.

"So here's what we did," says the detective. "When we took our crime scene photographs, in the kid's room—she was such a great mom, she had all these inspirational sayings and things like that hung up—I made sure those got into [the evidence shown to the jury], close-ups of those. So I could say at trial, 'Wait a minute. No. Here's the kind of mom she was.'"[19]

Photographs Can't Do It All

Crime scene photography can reveal other things, too—none of which make investigators happy. They can provide evidence of crucial errors in the way police investigators mishandle the evidence found at a crime scene. No case in recent years is as infamous for mishandling evidence than a famous double homicide that occurred in 1994. In that case, O.J. Simpson's ex-wife Nicole Brown Simpson and her friend Ronald Goldman were brutally stabbed to death outside her Los Angeles home.

Crime scene photographs show a number of things that were either ignored or missed by investigators. One was a piece of bloody paper on the ground near Nicole's head. Though the paper was there as photographers were documenting the scene, it was never processed. It was never taken to the crime lab and analyzed.

According to Michael Baden, former New York City chief medical examiner, the loss of any evidence weakens the case against any suspect. But a piece of paper that may have been in Nicole's hand as she died, or even dropped by her killer, may have been critically important. "Who knows what that piece of paper may have contained or where it went," Baden says. "Probably it left the scene on the sole of some unsuspecting detective's shoe."[20]

Blood Never Collected

That murder case, in which O.J. Simpson was charged and not convicted, became infamous for the mistakes and inconsistencies between crime scene photographs and evidence that was actually processed by forensic crews. Blood became another big problem—specifically the presence of blood on Nicole Simpson's back.

She had been found facedown, her throat slashed. She was lying in pools of her own blood. But the drops of blood in the middle of her back could not have been her own. Those who viewed the photographs said that by their shape, the drops had definitely come from someone else at the scene.

The importance of blood found at a crime scene is well known. A single drop of blood can be processed for DNA, a genetic code that is different for every human on Earth. Finding the DNA information from the blood on Simpson's back would have enabled investigators to order

A Los Angeles police detective points to a piece of paper found near Nicole Simpson's body. The paper, which was never processed, may have been a key piece of evidence.

DNA tests for the blood of a suspect. If it was a match, then it could be conclusively established that the suspect was present at the crime scene. However, in this case, the blood on Simpson's back was not collected and sampled.

That, explains former Michael Baden, was a critical error:

> Nobody lifted [the drops] from Nicole's skin to be analyzed and preserved. When the police completed their crime scene investigation, the coroner's people lifted Nicole's body and rolled her into a sheet and onto her back. . . . And as they were doing that, some of the blood leaking from her cut throat washed all the other spots of blood off her skin forever.[21]

Mistakes made in preserving important clues noticed in crime scene photographs of the Simpson-Goldman murders received wide attention. Fortunately, however, the discrepancies between crime photos and processed evidence are the exception, not the rule. The mistakes of the Simpson-Goldman case do point out how vital a role photography plays in the investigation of a crime. They are also a reminder of how important solid police work is in following through on the evidence revealed by those photographs.

CHAPTER 2

At the Scene of the Crime

The moment police receive a call about a serious crime such as a homicide, the dispatcher's first calls are to the detectives and the forensic crew—including the photographer. But it is the photographer who needs to gain access to the scene first. As forensic researcher David Fisher explains, "The very first thing that happens at a crime scene, before anything is touched, before the body is examined, before prints are developed, is that it is photographed."[22]

The first law enforcement personnel at the scene secure it—usually with crime scene tape to keep bystanders, reporters, and others out. In addition, one or more patrol officers are usually assigned to keep a physical presence at the scene, too. As mentioned earlier, it is vital that the scene be undisturbed. Theoretically, the photographer should be taking pictures of the scene as it was the second after the crime was committed.

"That's the Way It's Supposed to Work"

However, police and forensic workers know that it does not always work out that way. "The way it's supposed to work and the way it turns out are usually pretty different," says Dencell. "As a technician, I'm hoping the scene hasn't been disturbed before I photograph or collect evidence. But lots of times it is. And what may surprise people is that it's usually our people who are doing the disturbing."[23]

Crime scene experts say it is often the fire-rescue personnel, or the emergency medical technicians, who have been summoned to the scene by witnesses to the crime. "If the

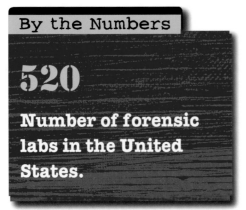

By the Numbers

520

Number of forensic labs in the United States.

victim is still alive, for example, that can be hard. I mean, it's good for the victim, but it means more people on the scene," says Bill Hinz. "Fire-rescue gets in there, and all of a sudden you've introduced a whole bunch of new items [at the scene] that weren't there at the time of the crime— dressings, bandage wrappers, stuff like that. It's their job to be there. But it is a problem for us."[24]

Another forensic tech agrees that it can be a problem, although he says it is not difficult to interpret evidence after medical teams have been there. "I can tell the difference between what was placed there by the medical team and what was placed there by the crooks," he says. "Usually you don't get little sterile pieces of paper that say Johnson and Johnson on them from the criminals breaking in."

What does worry him, he says, is how the emergency teams leave the scene before it is photographed. Often, there have been cases when medical teams have cleaned up their garbage and a cartridge case may inadvertently get stuck to a bandage or piece of adhesive tape. "We've actually gone through the bag of stuff that they've cleaned up and found evidentiary items," he says. "The only thing I ask the emergency team is: once they've done their action, don't move anything. If you have to pull a guy, move a guy, throw stuff around, leave it there."[25]

"You Know That One Cell Phone Commercial?"

Police, too, can sometimes interfere with photographers' work. "Detectives aren't supposed to start looking around until we're done," says Steve Banning. "Even though they know the possibilities of things getting moved around or lost." Banning says that police often enter the crime scene too early because they are impatient to get going on a case and are eager to get to get a look at the crime scene. Banning recalls:

> I remember this one scene I had down in a little town in southern Minnesota. A guy had wandered off and had gotten hypothermia [a condition where the body temperature gets too low] or something and died in a bean field. And this farmer was doing his stuff in the field and discovered the body. And we were called in to photograph and process the scene. I was the team leader then, and we hadn't looked at the scene yet.
>
> We told the investigators, "Look, we're going down to the scene and evaluate it. You guys wait here and we'll come back and tell you what we see, and then

Emergency personnel often arrive at a crime scene before the criminal investigation team. These first responders may inadvertently destroy crucial evidence.

Crime scene photographers must use a variety of cameras, lenses, and other related equipment, all of which they bring to a crime scene.

we'll tell you our own plan of action down there." So we started off down to the scene, and you know that one cell phone commercial—you know, where the guy is talking on his phone and that crowd of people, his network or whatever, they're following him? Well, that's what it was like. This whole group of investigators just falls in step behind us. And I'm thinking, what part of "You wait here" do you guys not understand?[26]

The Right Equipment

Once the forensic technicians get to the scene, they get a feeling for what sort of job it will be. They take out the equipment they need—and they carry a lot of it. Crime scene photographers have a variety of cameras. Most carry a 35-millimeter film camera and a variety of lenses—some for distant or general shots, others for showing the smallest details, such as the patterns of fingerprints. Photographers also have a powerful flash that can be attached to the camera or held separately so they can position the light in a way that best illuminates a particular piece of evidence.

If it is a homicide scene, many departments want the forensic technicians to use video, too, as they walk through the crime scene. Some departments prefer that the sound jacks are plugged, however. They do not want any background conversations to be audible. Hearing two detectives discussing their ideas of how the crime was committed, for example, could prejudice a jury if the videotape is used later in court.

On the other hand, some departments prefer to use the video with narration. They find it valuable for a technician to talk while walking through the scene for the first time, recording first impressions that could be helpful later. Says one technician:

> You look at a scene when you first see it and you think to yourself, "I'm going to remember this or that," or something strikes you about what you see. And it's like anything else, you might not remember that thought later, even though it seems so important and obvious to you at first. So having the sound on can be a really good thing.[27]

Camera Controversy

Most departments use digital cameras to photograph crime scenes, too—although their use has been the topic of a great deal of controversy. Digital images are not impressions caught on film, but rather bits of data. The images could conceivably be enhanced or manipulated using computer software such as Photoshop—and can end up revealing something completely different from the original images. That has forensic technicians and law enforcement worried that the validity of the digital photos presented in a court case could be questioned.

Crime scene photographer Monica Grafton illustrated this point to forensic researcher N.E. Genge. After taking several digital shots of Genge, Grafton attached the camera to her computer in the crime lab and in just moments created totally different images.

"What can be done is miraculous," reports Genge. "In moments, Monica alters the color of my hair, gives me a scar my twelve-year-old would envy, and turns my sedate blue jeans brilliant pink, and absolutely nothing in the background [of the images] has changed."[28]

No Worries

However, those worries have lessened in recent years. Photographers have learned to make it virtually impossible for their crime scene shots to be tampered with. Crime lab supervisor Bill Hinz explains:

> We prevent any of that. We come back into the office right after shooting a [crime] scene, download the images into our computer, and write it onto a CDR disc. The CDR is a one-time thing—you can only write on it the one time. There is no way you can do anything else with it. And that [disc] is essentially our negative, just as a film camera shot has a negative. So that solves that. No tampering, nothing.[29]

Such safekeeping technology has made a real difference. In 2005 fewer than 30 percent of police departments used digital because of concerns about its use in court. By 2007 more than 70 percent of departments—including the FBI, which had also resisted digital—issued digital cameras to their officers.

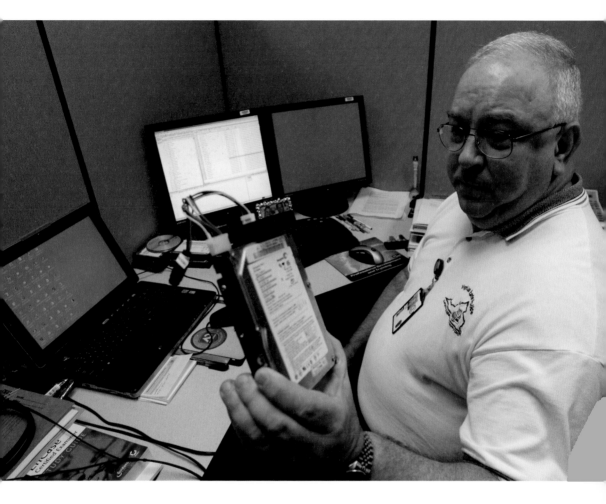

Forensic scientist Michael Calistro believes that is a good thing—for a number of reasons. He explains:

For one thing, digital is basically free. There's no film involved. So we go out to a scene and we tell our people, "Hey, blast away, shoot your brains out, as many photos as you can." Plus there's the advantage of storage. Film—it's bulky, you store the rolls in packets, and over time, that takes up huge amounts of space—whole rooms of stored evidence. With digital, it's on disk—tens of thousands of photos on a CD. I could put twenty years of [crime] scenes on my little shelf here.[30]

In a police computer evidence lab, an officer holds up a special hard drive used for safekeeping of data from digital cameras.

Scene or Scenes?

Another consideration in determining what equipment is needed is learning whether or not the crime is contained at one scene. Many people do not realize that a lot of crimes actually have multiple scenes, says Steve Banning. Many crime scenes are miles away from one another, and each one needs to be photographed and processed. Banning explains:

By the Numbers

16,137

Number of homicides in the United States in 2004.

I'll give you an example. I had a homicide down in Redwood Falls, in southern Minnesota, at an Indian reservation there. A body had been dumped by the river. They'd taken the victim's car and burned it. So that's two scenes right there—the body at the river and the car. And then there's the house they'd originally started beating the guy up, that's another scene. And you've got to do them all. It could take days and days to do it all.[31]

In the case of the Redwood Falls murder, Banning used a camera at the river scene to take photos from a helicopter hovering overhead. He says:

At that scene, I could take lots of photos showing stuff I couldn't see from the ground—as far as how it all related. I could see the spot on the river where the body had been dumped, and the little access roads and paths in the area. That could help later in figuring out how the vehicle got to that spot—it was pretty remote. And the aerial photography was really necessary to tie it all together.[32]

On the other hand, a crime such as a drive-by shooting, with multiple witnesses on a city street, is limited—not only to one scene, but by the number of photographs needed. Bill Hinz explains:

You don't have a lot of evidence at a scene like that. You got a body, of course, and because the shooter probably used a semi-automatic, like in a lot of this kind of shooting, you're not going to see casings lying on the street. So there's no way of gathering a lot of evidence. Not a lot of photographs, not a lot to document. Instead, in a case like that, you will need to rely more on witnesses than forensic evidence.[33]

Fragile Evidence First

Although individual photographers may have their own preferred methods of documenting a scene, they all agree on some things. One of those agreed-upon things is what

Photographers work quickly to capture criminal evidence that will likely disappear. Fragile evidence is always photographed first.

needs to be shot first. And, says one forensic expert, it is not what people often assume—a dead body. "The body is the last thing we're going to look at," he says. "Once the paramedics, or whoever, have determined that the victim can't be saved, there's no point in rushing up to the body. It's not going anywhere."[34]

Instead, it is the most fragile evidence that is documented immediately. Anything that is likely to disappear quickly— because of weather or exposure to the elements—is considered fragile. So is a piece of evidence on the victim's body, such as hairs or other trace evidence, that may be lost once the victim is moved by the medical examiner's crew.

Any fire scene that is suspected to be arson is often completely fragile. "If you've got a structure that's even partially destroyed by fire," says arson investigator Sean McKenna, "and it's vital to get the pictures taken and the evidence be photographed and processed right away. The inside, where the evidence is, is exposed to the elements—you might have a roof that's partly gone, an outside wall gone—so you have to get what you can from the scene quick."[35]

Overall Shots

Once the more immediate photography is done, the photographer begins methodically to document the scene. Steve Banning says that photographers tend to work from the outside perimeters toward the inside.

"Let's say you've got a homicide at a residence," he says. "The first shots are overall shots. The first would be one of the area the house or apartment is in. You'd get a shot of the street sign, so the location is clearly shown. Then you walk around the whole house or apartment, taking shots all around."[36]

Banning says it is very important to document all entry points of the residence, too. "You don't know how the person got into the residence—whether they came in the front door, or pried open a window or the back door, or even through a garage entry. And you want to make sure you document any

Faces in the Crowd

Although fragile evidence such as outdoor shoe impressions at the scene must be photographed quickly, there is another shot that crime scene photographers at a suspected arson fire say must be taken quickly—the crowd. Many arsonists enjoy watching the fires they have set and will stand with a crowd of onlookers as firefighters and other emergency personnel rush to the blaze. For that reason, crime scene photographers will routinely take video of the crowd and may later compare those faces with those seen at other suspicious fires. The photographer also may be asked by investigators to photograph all license plates of cars parked within a block or two of the scene, just in case one of them belongs to the arsonist.

driveway or alley near the residence, and show where it is in relation to the building."[37]

He says that like everything else at a scene, it is impossible to know for certain what will be important to investigators. "Take all the pictures you can," he says. "If you make a mistake, make the one of taking too many shots, rather than not enough."[38]

Covering Up

Once the outside shots are complete, the photographer goes inside. Photographers put on protective clothing at a scene—sometimes at an outdoor scene, but always when they are shooting photos indoors. "Typically, we'd wear gloves and sort of coveralls," says Dencell. "And hair coverings. The idea is you don't want anything that belongs to you—your hair, the cat hair on your sweater, fibers from your coat, stuff like that—to get into the crime scene."[39]

Becoming a Crime Scene Photographer/ Forensic Technician

Job Description:

The crime scene photographer in most police departments throughout the United States is one aspect of the job of crime scene analyst. This person responds to crime scenes and has duties including documenting (either by videotaping, still photography, or both) the crime scene, as well as detecting and gathering evidence to be taken later to the crime lab. In many jurisdictions, these technicians also process the evidence back at the crime lab.

Education:

Must have had college-level courses, or their equivalent, in chemistry, biology, photographic techniques, fingerprinting techniques, and the use of alternative lighting sources.

Salary:

A crime scene technician usually earns a yearly salary ranging from $45,000 to $67,000.

Dencell says that no matter how neat and clean a technician is, he or she will leave some trace behind unless protective coverings are used. He explains:

> That's Locard's principle, the one you learn about first when you are starting out. Every contact between person and a scene, there will be an exchange of trace. So you may leave a fiber or one of your hairs or piece of lint. And you bring something out of the scene, too. Usually it's too small for most people to even notice. But that's the stuff techs look for at a scene.[40]

Dencell says such transfer is good in that the murderer or intruder has left a clue. "But if [the trace evidence] is from one of the techs, that's lot of wasted time," he says. "Like if techs process cat hairs at a murder, they need to assume that if there's no cat on premises, the hair might have been carried there by the unsuspecting perpetrator. Best that they don't have to waste their time processing stuff from one of their own who didn't cover up."[41]

Moving in Closer

Inside a crime scene, photographers must be as methodical as they were

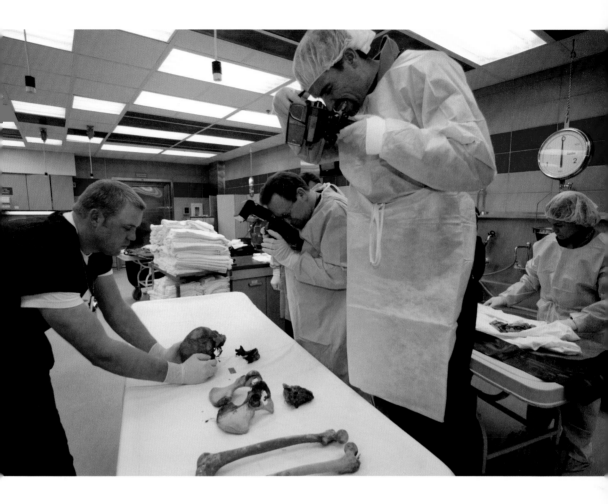

when doing the overall outside shots. Many experienced photographers find a central point and start taking shots of the room with that point as their starting place. That way, they do not miss any area of the scene.

A photographer takes shots of each room in such a way that the photographs overlap. That way, the viewer later can see the connection between them. If the kitchen connects to a bathroom, for example, the shot of the kitchen can show the entry to the bathroom.

If there is evidence there, the photographer will take mid-range shots, showing how that piece of evidence relates to an object in the room. If there is a gun on the floor near

In an effort to prevent contamination of evidence, most crime scene photographers cover their bodies and hair with protective clothing.

a coffee table, for instance, it is important for the mid-range shot to show the gun in relation to the table. And once that is done, the photographer can concentrate on taking more specific shots showing the minute details of any evidence at the scene.

Taking a Closer Look

Photographer Steve Banning says he routinely goes through the scene more than once. He explains:

> I don't have to get everything the first time. I go through the first time, just taking photos of what I saw when I got there—how it looked. I do the rooms, and any mid-range shots. And then as I progress, I start finding evidence I didn't see at first, and I take more photographs, and more mid-range shots. So you have the initial photos, and then you always have the camera around to take any additional ones.[42]

Photographers should look not just for obvious evidence, such as bloodstains or a weapon. There may be other, more subtle items in a room that could provide investigators with insight about the victim, too. Taking photos in the victim's bathroom of the specific items in the medicine cabinet might help. So would books or other reading material on a table or nightstand.

Any evidence that appears to be directly related to the homicide—a knife on the floor, a bloody area on the rug, and so on—needs to be photographed with a common, everyday item that can show its general size. "You can use a quarter, a book of matches, or a small ruler," says Amy. "It just gives a sense of scale when looking at the photograph."[43]

Lighting

All photography requires light, but that can be a problem at many scenes. Different types of light show up on camera in various colors. Incandescent light shows up yellow. Fluorescent lights, like those in many offices, gives a green cast to the picture. "It's a trick to learn at first," says Bill Hinz, "because when you're getting the shot, you don't see that color. Our eyes don't see the green or yellow light, but the cameras do."[44]

The light needs to be balanced, so that the light is white—and therefore is an accurate image of what the eye would see. Photographers learn to make choices with the film they use, or filters that can control the light in a particular shot.

Worse than colored light, however, is no light at all. Pictures can only form on film when light bounces off the object being photographed and hits the film. That causes a chemical change on the film, which produces an image. But at an outdoor

Painting with Light

Another interesting technique is used by crime scene photographers who lack the light needed for nighttime shots in a large area. It is called "painting with light," and it is especially helpful if a photographer is working alone on a scene and cannot use multiple flashes.

Basically, the photographer opens the camera's shutter so that instead of opening and closing quickly, as in most shots, it remains open as it is focused on the object. Steve Banning, who learned this technique at a special FBI class, says:

Usually it's a big object, like a car. You have the camera mounted on a tripod, because you're not going to be holding it. What you do is walk around the object you're shooting with your handheld flash, and just keep setting off the flash in different areas near the car. And what that does, when the flash keeps going off, it lights up that segment of the car. When you get that film or digital image later, the whole vehicle will be well-lit.

Steve Banning, personal interview, November 9, 2004, St. Paul, MN.

nighttime scene, no real light is bouncing off the object. "You have flash, but it doesn't do much," Hinz says. "Streetlights affect it, car headlights affect it. And it's nowhere near as powerful as what you need." Hinz says photographers use multiple flashes when possible, or more powerful light sources called strobes. "But even that isn't always enough," he says.

Hinz says many crime scene crews call the fire department in such cases. "We get them to send a truck with the big floodlights," he says. "That can really light up the area, so we can get our shots. That's great when a handheld flash or a strobe just won't do the job."[45]

"Whatever It Takes"

Most important, say photographers, is that one must be adaptable—especially in getting the initial shots at a new crime scene. Says Steve Banning:

> Whatever it takes to get an accurate shot to document [a crime scene], you do. It isn't always easy, and sometimes you may look back later and wish you'd known about a certain technique at the time. But you do the best you can. I think that ultimately, you just keep remembering how important your job is in an investigation. And if you do your job right, it can lead to a criminal's arrest and conviction.[46]

CHAPTER 3

All in the Details

The photographer must take other pictures before the crime scene is completely processed. These are detailed images of clues that a criminal may not even realize he or she has left at the scene. But they may be the very bits of evidence that will lead to that person's arrest.

Patterns of Ridges

Fingerprints are one of the most important types of evidence found at a scene. And because fingerprints need to be photographed, they are among the most important images—and often the most difficult ones—a crime scene photographer will take in relation to any case.

Fingerprints are the tiny patterns made by the various ridges that make up the pads of the fingers. Ridges are important, for they give the fingertips the ability to grip something smooth. Without ridges the fingers would be completely smooth, without friction.

The ridges form patterns that are different for every person. No two people on Earth have the same fingerprints. Even identical twins do not have the same fingerprints. And the pattern does not change. From the time one is born to the day that person dies, the fingerprints remain the same.

Visible Prints at a Crime Scene

Sometimes fingerprints at a scene are visible. For instance, a 2001 robbery in Chicago was solved because the thief had eaten at McDonald's shortly before breaking into a home. Though he did not realize it at the time, he had ketchup on one of his fingers, and an alert photographer at the scene took a picture of a fingerprint in ketchup on the outside windowsill.

This kind of a fingerprint is called a patent print. Patent prints are visible after a person's fingers have had contact with a substance that can color them, such as ink, dirt, or blood. When that person touches a surface at the crime scene, his or her fingerprints become noticeable.

Another visible print is called an impression print, or plastic print. It is created when a person touches a soft surface, such as putty, wax, or soap. The ridges of the fingertip actually embed themselves in the soft surface, creating a three-dimensional fingerprint. Crime scene worker Kari Day-Wells once found the only clear print left at a crime scene in a piece of chocolate. The intruder had spotted the box of Christmas candy and decided to help himself. However, the piece he bit into was not to his liking, and he put it back in the box. "The suspect touched nothing else," she says, "but was caught because he didn't like nuts."[47]

By the Numbers

60,000

Number of finger-prints that can be checked per second using AFIS.

Photographing Fingerprints

The most important aspect of the fingerprint, obviously, is the tiny details that make it different from other fingerprints. That means that the photographer must get as much of the fingerprint as possible into the picture, so the minute ridge pattern is visible.

There are three important steps in this process. The first is making sure that the lens is one specifically used for close-up work, rather than one used for overall shots of the crime scene. A close-up lens can usually be attached to the same camera used for other crime scene photographs. Another important piece of equipment is a tripod. This is a three-legged stand on which the camera is mounted. Amy notes:

You don't want the camera to move, not even a little bit. And working with a [close-up] lens, any movement can affect the shot.

Sometimes you move a little, not even noticing you are. Like if you are breathing heavy after climbing up four flights of stairs to a crime scene, your heart is beating fast, and that causes the camera to kind of jump a little. Anytime you're shooting a piece of evidence like a fingerprint or a footprint or something, the whole point is detail. And if [the camera] moves, even a little bit, you can lose that detail to blurring. That's why you need the tripod.[48]

Lighting, too, is an important consideration for photographing a fingerprint. Notes photographer Steve Banning:

Before a fingerprint is lifted at a crime scene, the print must first be photographed up close. Note the ruler in the lower right, used for establishing scale.

In some crime scene photos, the problem is often not having enough light. With fingerprints, it's usually the opposite. If you use a flash the same way you use it for other shots, you get too much light. It blows out the print. Instead, you can hold the flash off to one side, or reflect it off another object, so you have enough light without bleaching out the detail you need.[49]

Photographing What Cannot Be Seen

The most common fingerprints found at a scene are neither patent nor impression prints. They are called latent prints, for they are virtually invisible to the naked eye. "That's a good thing, in a way," says Dencell. "Because the bad guys are usually unaware they have left a latent print—even if they are trying to be very careful not to touch anything. They can't see them, so sometimes when they're cleaning up a scene, they don't get them all."[50]

Latent prints are made by the naturally occurring sweat and oils coming from the skin's pores to the ridges of the fingertips. And when that person touches an object, the pattern of the ridges is left on that object. Of course, a latent print cannot be documented until it is made visible, and that is the biggest challenge to the photographer.

The first step, however, is often to use a light to see if prints even exist on a certain object. That can be done with a laser, a high-energy light source used by forensic teams. If prints exist on a surface at the crime scene, the photographer or technician determines what will best work to make the prints visible. That usually involves using powders or one of a wide range of chemicals that can bring out the latent print's detail and make it easy to see and process.

For example, if the print is on a smooth surface, such as a table or countertop, one can apply special fingerprint powder that sticks to the sweats and oils of the print. After lightly applying the powder with a special brush, the excess powder can be gently blown away, leaving a print that can be easily seen. Then the print can be "lifted" by applying a piece of clear sticky tape to the powdered print and carefully removing it. The image of the print is placed on a clear plastic card and is labeled and filed for later examination.

Before the print is lifted, however, it is photographed. This is a necessary step, for sometimes the lifting does not work well and a print is damaged during the process. The photograph

First Impression

Processing and lifting prints of any sort is often difficult and requires a lot of practice. In this excerpt from N.E. Genge's The Forensic Casebook, *forensic investigator Paul Gaetan recalls the disastrous results of his first attempt to lift a print after photographing it.*

I wasn't a print person, just winging it, but there was no one else available and I figured something—no matter how bad—was better than nothing. Even a shoe size would help, right? The print was an oily substance, but I didn't know what. I waited for it to dry a bit, then blew black powder over it and blew away the excess. The lifting material was overlapping tape that I affixed to a piece of white cardstock and shipped off to the lab down south, thinking, "That wasn't so hard." . . . .

The guy who opened it had me on the phone in no time, gave me an earful on my "technique." The "oil" wasn't oil, exactly. It was brake fluid or something. It melted the tape and we got nothing but a soggy mess for our trouble. Thank God for photos. I think he would have flown up and shaken me if I hadn't taken photos!

Quoted in N.E. Genge, *The Forensic Casebook*. New York: Ballantine, 2002, pp. 61–62.

provides an important backup that can be used later when comparing the latent print with one of a suspect.

"Only One Print"

A police department screen shot of a digital fingerprint demonstrates the complex patterns and whorls that each fingerprint possesses uniquely.

Sometimes, an important case is solved because of a photograph of a single powdered print. Minneapolis forensic scientist and photographer Michael Calistro recalls the case where he was looking for fingerprints of a car thief who had caused the death of an elderly woman. When the car was recovered later, police were hoping to get a fingerprint of the man.

"We were looking for places on the car that a person would touch—side and rearview mirrors, steering wheel, and so on—

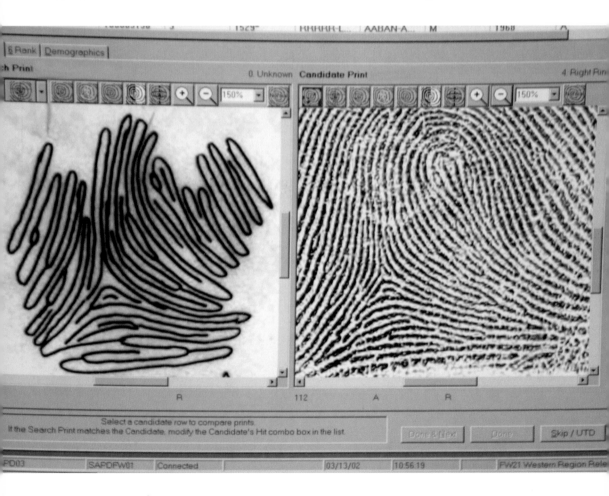

with no luck," Calistro says, "but finally we were lucky. We found a little one-inch by one-inch square of plastic in the middle of the steering wheel—the horn button."

Calistro says that he took the photograph of the fingerprint after dusting it with black powder—but could not use his tripod to steady the camera. He says:

> A lot of times you improvise. The surface was at an angle, so using the tripod wasn't an option. In situations like these, you want to lean against something sturdy—kind of make yourself into a human tripod, so you don't have any movement at all. That works—and it did this time, too. We were able to get a clear shot. The print belonged to the bad guy, and he was caught because of it.[51]

By the Numbers

0

How many people share the same fingerprint.

Into the Lab

While a photographer takes some shots of latent prints at the crime scene, much of the fingerprint photography is done back at the crime lab. "Some things you pretty much have to do at the scene," says Amy. "Counters, sections of walls, bathroom fixtures are things you aren't going to be moving. But smaller items of interest—a weapon or something else the bad guy might have left at the scene—we bring back. And we have lots of things [at the lab] that we can use to make [latent prints] visible."[52]

Fourty-Five Choices

David Peterson is a fingerprint expert with Minnesota's Bureau of Criminal Apprehension. He says that the choice of what he uses to develop a particular print so it can be photographed depends on the surface. Paper, for example, requires something other than fingerprint powder. Peterson says:

The thing is, the oils, the amino acids, the stuff that makes up a fingerprint, it soaks into the paper, rather than stay on the surface, so dusting . . . isn't very efficient. We get prints that are far more clear if we use chemicals, and we've got lots of choices—in all, forty-five different chemicals for different situations. Often you try one, if it doesn't work, well, you try something else that's more sensitive.[53]

Many photographers use ninhydrin, a chemical that can react with heat to make latent prints visible on paper. After spraying the surface of the paper with the ninhydrin, a technician puts the paper in a microwave oven. After it is heated for several minutes, the prints will appear in a bright pinkish-purple color. Then the photographer can get a close-up image of the print. By using a small tripod, like the ones used at a crime scene, and a special lens used strictly for close-up work, the photographer can keep the camera steady while making certain that the shot will be focused and clear.

Into the System

Once the fingerprint is photographed, investigators begin the process of identifying who it belongs to. If there is a known suspect in the case, that person is fingerprinted and a photograph is made from that, too. Then the two photographs are enlarged so the details are easy to see. The examiner can then decide if there is a match.

If not, there is still a way of identifying the print, and that uses photography, too. It is called the Automated Fingerprint Identification System, or AFIS. Introduced and maintained by the FBI, AFIS enables police to compare an unidentified print with those of millions of other prints from all over the United States.

An examiner takes the print found at the scene to the AFIS machine, which has a camera attached to it. The camera takes a photo of the print and displays it on a large screen.

The examiner enlarges it so the tiniest details are visible. The examiner plots out certain key characteristics in an area of the fingerprint that may make it different from others. "The machine calculates the position of the minutiae [tiny details of the print] in relation to one another," explains Bill Hinz. "And then we send it—enter it into the system."

The AFIS system flags anything in its system that matches the plotted minutiae the examiner has entered on the computer. "We usually ask for the top 25 most likely matches," says Hinz. "And then an examiner sits down and decides whether any of them are a match. That examiner looks at each of the print photos sent by the system, and compares it to the photo of our print. If it's a match, it's a human who makes that decision, not a machine."[54]

The AFIS database run by the FBI employs sophisticated technology to store millions of fingerprints. The system is used for comparing prints.

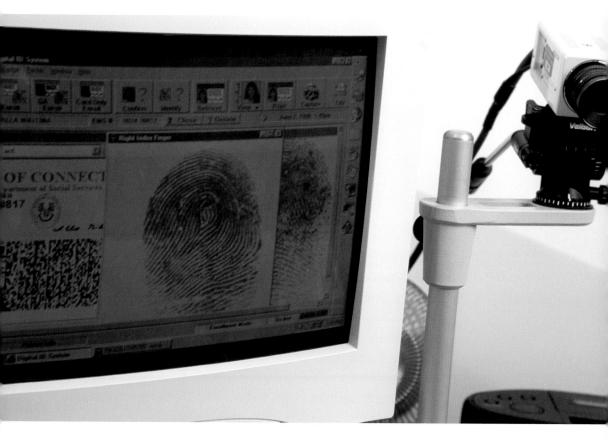

Impressions

Fingerprints are not the only detailed photographs taken by the photographer. Impressions can also be highly valuable evidence in solving a case. Automobile tires are an excellent example. Although it may seem that they are all pretty much the same, says Steve Banning, a closer inspection shows that they are actually very different. "They differ in width, a lot of features that tire manufacturers add to reduce noise, to make the tire last longer, to give it more stability on slippery roads, things like that. If you take a real close look, you'll see a real variety in the details."[55]

In addition to having hundreds of combinations of different features from the manufacturer, tires wear differently. Because cars are seldom aligned perfectly, tires get different amounts of wear on the edges, rather than just in the middle. In addition, the tire picks up debris from the road, and that can become embedded in the tread—a rock or a nail, for example, which will leave an unusual pattern.

Tires become almost as individualized as fingerprints, and that can make them very helpful evidence. If a tire tread can be photographed and processed, it can be found in one of several tire databases used by law enforcement—databases that contain thousands of different makes, models, and sizes of tires. If investigators can identify the specific kind of tire from an impression, they will look closely at any suspect whose vehicle is fitted with those tires.

Photographing Tire Impressions

Just as with fingerprints, tire impressions are processed as well as photographed. In the case of three-dimensional tire impressions—those left in mud, snow, or sand, for example—technicians will attempt to make a casting of the print. This is like a plaster mold of the impression. On the other hand, if a tire mark is one-dimensional—a mark on the road left from a tire that is muddy or oily, technicians lift the print, much as they do a latent fingerprint. And though in most cases, making

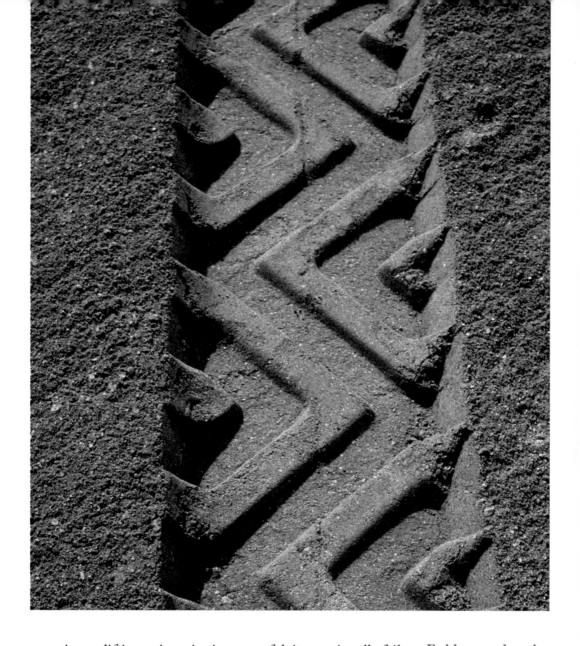

a casting or lifting a tire print is successful, it occasionally fails, and evidence can be destroyed in the process. For this reason, the photographer must take pictures first.

Banning says that for taking impression prints, the right light is the key. He explains:

> You can't take them straight on. Especially with something that's three-dimensional. You want to see the depth, and if you take [a photo] head on, you won't

Evidence such as tire tracks or imprints are photographed first due to their fragile nature. Tire prints such as the one shown here are unique.

really see the treads. So you take the flash attachment off the camera, hold it out to the side, like at a 45-degree angle. That's called oblique lighting, and that will make all the difference in the world for a tread. That highlights the ridges, and that's important for the investigators who are going to try to match this with a suspect's tire.[56]

Some photographers like to use orange spray paint to bring out the details of a faint tire or footwear impression. They hold the can about 10 inches (25cm) above the impression and spray the paint outward, rather than aim it directly at the print. The spray can fall gently on the higher points of the impression. "This will make the photo of the impression jump off the page," write forensic researchers Jarrett Hallcox and Amy Welch, "without damaging the impression itself."[57]

"He Saved Eight Bucks, but Went to Prison for Life"

In her book *Every Contact Leaves a Trace*, Connie Fletcher interviewed a homicide detective who solved a murder because of tire tread marks left at the scene. A woman's ex-boyfriend was jealous, and he took the woman and her new boyfriend to a park. The ex ended up shooting the new boyfriend, and he coerced the woman to stay in the relationship with him and not tell what had happened.

Interestingly, the killer knew something about crime scene investigation. He was worried that when the police found the body, they would see the tire tracks of his girlfriend's car and use that evidence to tie the murder back to him. The detective says that is exactly what happened—the police processed and photographed the tire impressions at the scene, and even though the killer had tried to outsmart them, he was not quite smart enough. The detective explains:

What he did was, he took a jackknife and punctured all four tires, and then went to [his girlfriend] and said, "Honey, the tires are leaking. We should get some more tires." He went to Kmart with her credit card and bought four new tires. But then he was so cheap he didn't want to pay the tire recycling fee. He took all four old tires, left the tires near the back porch.

Couple days later, we caught up with him. We looked at the car and saw that the tire pattern did not match the impressions from the scene. But then we found the four tires, all punctured. And one of the tire impressions matched the impression from the scene. He saved eight bucks, but he went to prison for life.[58]

Tracing Footsteps

Photographs of shoeprints are just as important as those of tire treads. In fact, many forensic experts believe that the soles of people's shoes are even more distinctive than the tires on their car. "Take your shoes off and look at the bottoms of your shoes," challenges one footwear expert. "What you'll see, in addition to the general wear patterns, are a whole bunch of unique, random marks, scratches, gouges. . . . I can take a police department with five hundred police officers that all wear the same boot, and we can differentiate each pair from all the others."[59]

That is good news for investigators, for shoe prints are common clues at crime scenes. In a 2000 New York City burglary,

Photographing a Footprint Impression

1 Lightly spray orange paint in the air about 10 inches (25cm) above the footprint, not directly at it.

2 Place a footwear scale near the impression (but not touching it), so that it is evident to the viewer how large the footprint really is.

3 Set the tripod directly over the print, and mount the camera so that it is pointing straight down.

4 The photographer or a helper can use oblique lighting, at a 45-degree angle at the side of the impression, so that the three-dimensional details of the print can be seen.

5 Press the button on the camera.

a back door to an electronics store had been kicked in. Police found a dusty shoe print on the door, and forensic crews photographed it. Says Dencell:

> It was a pretty good print. It was a Nike shoe, size 12. We could tell that because of the ruler the photographer used for scale. And the shoe had a lot of horizontal cut marks on the left heel, for whatever reason. Anyway, it turned out to be an important lead, because there had been several burglaries of electronics stores in the past month or two. Police in another precinct had already talked to one guy. They didn't have any real proof, but suspected he was in on it.

This exhibit of shoe print comparison was used at the trial of O.J. Simpson. Each person's shoe print is one of a kind.

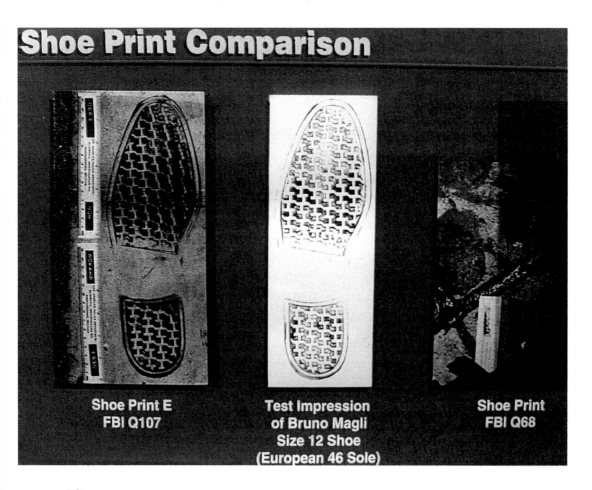

Shoe Print Comparison

**Shoe Print E
FBI Q107**

**Test Impression
of Bruno Magli
Size 12 Shoe
(European 46 Sole)**

**Shoe Print
FBI Q68**

Creative Ideas and Solving Crimes

Sometimes the best evidence at a crime scene is invisible—and therefore, is never gathered or documented by forensic technicians. In a recent series of burglaries in Cedar Falls, Iowa, one detective had been frustrated by the lack of clues. Although they had a suspect, they had absolutely no evidence to tie him to the burglaries, until the detective finally recovered a flashlight left behind by the thieves after another burglary. Unfortunately, he found no latent prints at all on the flashlight, and it seemed that he was no better off than before. However, he had an idea—surely when the batteries in the flashlight were last changed, the thieves would not have been wearing gloves.

The detective carefully removed the batteries and treated them with superglue fumes—often used to bring out prints on shiny surfaces. Using a special alternative light source, he was then able to photograph several fingerprints on the batteries. The fingerprints matched a suspect, and the case was solved.

Anyway, it turned out he wore shoes that totally fit the photo we had of our burglar's [shoe print]. I mean, how many people would have those same shoes with those weird cut marks? At first he denied being there at all, but that didn't last long. Then he told the detectives that he was there, but didn't do anything. But that didn't hold up either. He just couldn't explain away the footprint on the door. And that ended up being a big part of nailing the guy.[60]

What the Photographs Tell

The photography that clearly shows a fingerprint, a tire tread, or a shoe print is very important to many criminal cases. But it is also important to understand that in itself, such evidence is only a part of the case. Says Michael Calistro:

> For instance, a fingerprint is only a fingerprint. What we do [as photographers] is to document that a piece of evidence was there, and often to make it more visible to the eye.
>
> We aren't saying that the person whose fingerprint it is, is necessarily guilty. A fingerprint doesn't prove that. But it does prove that he or she was there, at that scene. If you say you weren't there and I have a photo of your fingerprint that I took at the scene, what that says is that you aren't telling the truth. Why? I don't know. But I know the investigator will want to find out.[61]

CHAPTER 4

The Body as a Crime Scene

The physical location where a crime took place can tell a story by the evidence discovered and photographed at the scene. However, in some crimes, such as homicide or assault, the body itself can provide a wealth of information. In fact, investigators think of the victim of such a crime as a special crime scene—with evidence of its own that must be photographed and documented. This evidence may provide important clues that help investigators solve the crime.

"There is all kinds of evidence on the body," says Amy, a forensic technician. "From bloodstains and bullet holes to material under the fingernails if the victim fought off their attacker. Bruising, knife wounds, fibers and material that may have transferred from the murderer to the victim—there's a lot of possibilities for forensic crews."[62]

The Body at the Scene

Photographers take a range of photos of the victim at the scene of a homicide. They take shots from all angles, to make certain they document exactly where the body is at the scene. Just as photographers need to make certain a weapon is photographed in relation to some other object at the scene, it is important that they document the exact spot the body was found—outside near a street sign, inside next to the dining room table, and so on.

It is important to provide a number of shots of the face, too—full-face as well as profile shots. This is done so that if there is any question about who the victim is, there will be photographs that provide an identifiable likeness. One Los Angeles victim had no identification on his body when he

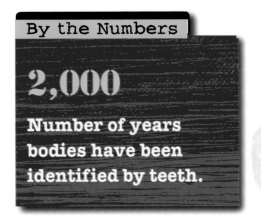

By the Numbers

2,000

Number of years bodies have been identified by teeth.

was stabbed to death in 2004. One of the photographer's pictures taken at the scene showed a Navy anchor tattoo on the man's forearm, with the name of the ship on which he served. That information helped investigators to learn his name.

The Wrong-Way Knife

Photographs of the body at a homicide scene can also reveal information that the scene itself was staged, or manufactured, by the criminal. One investigator recalls going to a scene where a husband had shot his wife. The man claimed that she had tried to stab him and the shooting was self-defense.

"But," says the investigator, "there were a couple things that just didn't make sense. There was a knife in her hand. But it was in the wrong direction to be used as a stabbing-type instrument. It was very apparent that he had placed the knife in her hand after he shot her and, probably in his panic, he had it facing the wrong way."[63]

Photographs taken at the scene not only documented the knife's position for detectives, but also provided evidence that would be important to show the jury at the man's trial. It was not self-defense at all, and instead he would be tried for murder.

Bloody Confusion

Once the body has been photographed, forensic crews give the medical team the go-ahead to remove it—usually to the medical examiner, where it will be examined closely for more clues. "Unless the victim is slightly breathing," says one technician, "we never let them move the body until we can get a good look at it."[64]

Steve Banning agrees, and says that problems can occur when the body is moved before the photographer gets the shots of it. "We had one scene, a really bloody one," he says.

"And when the EMTs hauled the victim out, that person had been bleeding. So anyway, when we start processing it, we see these blood droplets going out the door."[65]

Banning says that was confusing to detectives as well as the forensic crews. "Well, we were wondering, okay, was the guy who shot the victim hurt, too? Was that his blood from when he was running out the door? We had no idea that the blood came from the victim being taken out on a stretcher. We

All criminal investigators at the scene wear protective clothing to keep the site uncontaminated.

"In the Middle of a Horror Movie"

One of the most dramatic cases of the use of Luminol in an investigation was the 1992 murder of Caren Campano in Oklahoma City. Her husband, Chris, admitted that they had argued before she disappeared, but denied any involvement in her disappearance. There was some evidence of blood on a rug, but police know that people cut themselves all the time. The presence of a bit of blood does not mean someone was murdered.

The proof came when they used Luminol. The chemical works best when it is absolutely dark, so police waited for a moonless night, so any glowing would be easy to see. What they saw astonished them. "There was so much blood in the room—invisible to the naked eye, but glowing after the Luminol treatment," reports forensic researcher Paul Dowling, "that people could actually see each other. It was clear that blood had been everywhere—on the walls, the ceiling, the doors. One veteran police officer later said it was like being 'in the middle of a horror movie.'"

Quoted in Paul Dowling, *The Official Forensic Files Casebook*. New York: iBooks, 2004, p. 15.

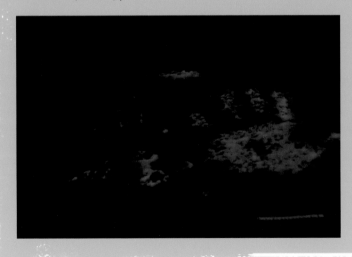

This crime lab photo shows the eerie glow of Luminol as blood reacts with the chemical.

didn't know what happened at the scene—we had no photos before the guy was moved."[66]

"Blood Was Something You Cleaned Up"

But when all goes well at a scene and the protocol is followed correctly, bloodstains found there can yield an amazing amount of information. It was not always that way, however. "In the beginning," notes one technician, "blood was something you cleaned up."[67] But no more. In fact, after the body has been taken from the scene, each and every bloodstain, no matter how small, will be photographed and documented because of the valuable information about the crime that it can provide.

For example, experts know that in many cases, the trail of blood can show exactly where the victim was first struck, stabbed, or shot. "In a very bloody scene, it's typically the area with the least blood that is the place where [the victim] first was attacked," says Amy. "A wound tends to bleed more after that. In cases where the victim tries to keep moving after that, he'll bleed more and more. You can virtually see his movement through the scene."[68]

The individual drops of blood are critically important, too. The shape of each one can tell investigators the angle at which it hit. For instance, a drop of blood falling from directly over a smooth surface will be perfectly round. If it falls at an angle, it is more elliptical—the shape of an elongated circle with flatter sides. And looking at that elliptical drop, an expert can tell from which direction the drop was traveling.

The size of the drops is important, too. The smaller the drops, the faster they were moving when they hit the surface. Large drops usually result from low-impact injuries, such as a punch. Middle-sized drops may be the result of a beating with a blunt object, or even a stabbing. Droplets from a gunshot wound, where the blood is traveling very rapidly, are so tiny they appear almost like a mist—each is less than 1/25 of an inch (6.35mm) in diameter.

Suicide? Homicide?

Although blood spatter is almost always viewed as a crime-fighting tool, sometimes photographs of blood spatter can show investigators that a crime did not take place. That was the case during a summer heat wave in Texas, where a man was found hanging in his home. The body was not discovered until two or three days afterward, and it had begun decomposing.

Detectives called to the scene noticed right away that something seemed odd. The walls and ceiling of the room in which the body was found were covered with tiny droplets of blood. It appeared at first as though the man had been savagely beaten and then hung. Forensic examiner Linda Harrison viewed the photographs taken at the scene and at first agreed with the detectives—before she realized what the blood actually was. Harrison explains:

> When I first took a look at the photographs of the walls and ceiling, it did look like it might be blood spatter. But as I looked a little more carefully, I could see that it wasn't. What it was all over those walls was fly excrement. Flies had been feeding on the body, then landing on the walls and ceiling with blood on their legs and excreting the blood they'd digested.[69]

The tip-off, said Harrison, was a photograph of a lightbulb that had been left on. "There wasn't a spot on it," she recalls. "The flies hadn't gone near it because it was too hot for them. If we'd been dealing with blood spatter, we certainly would have found some there. We couldn't tell [detectives] for sure that this was a suicide, but we could tell them that the scene wasn't the result of a beating."[70]

Finding Invisible Blood

Some blood evidence at a scene can be latent, or invisible, just as fingerprints can be. This happens because people try to clean up blood to hide that a murder has taken place. In such cases, the killer moves the body and may tell investigators that the person is simply missing. The presence of blood can contradict that story, so the killer tries everything he or she can to make the scene spotless.

However, forensic experts say that it is virtually impossible to get rid of all signs of blood, no matter how clean the room may appear. Dencell recalls:

A forensic lab technician uses a cotton swab to detect the presence of blood in crime scene evidence.

I've had a [forensic] team leader who had a nose like a bloodhound—no pun intended. He could walk into a scene and whenever he smelled Lysol or some cleaner —especially one with bleach—he'd zone in on it. He figured if the guy had been cleaning recently with bleach, it was most likely to get rid of blood. He was very suspicious that way—he asked me once, "Think about it, if your wife had gone missing and had been gone for days, would doing deep cleaning on the carpet and walls be the first thing on your to-do list?"[71]

But even with powerful cleaners, say investigators, blood is virtually impossible to clean up completely. It can drip down behind floorboards and under rug pads, and minute amounts can collect in the tile grout in a bathroom. In order for the blood to be photographed, technicians use a substance called Luminol. It is a combination of several chemicals and water, and when it comes in contact with the iron found in blood, it will fluoresce, or glow. Interestingly, the photography process must be done quickly, for the glow only lasts about thirty seconds. But while it is glowing, the Luminol can enable the crime scene photographer to see not only large stains, but also the spatter at the scene.

Photographer Steve Banning explains:

I've had cases where the bad guys have tried to clean up the trunk of a car after they killed someone and transported the body. Whether it's because of the dark carpeting in there or whatever, you don't see any blood when you look at the trunk. But investigators suspect it's there, so we spray with Luminol and we find it and photograph it. Again, the idea is to document the presence of blood when the case goes to trial.[72]

To the Medical Examiner

Once a body is removed from the scene of a homicide, or from the scene of any suspicious death, it is taken to the medical

examiner. In most cases, a medical examiner is a doctor whose specialty is determining the cause of death—whether suicide, homicide, or natural causes. And as the examination of the body is conducted, photography is a key part of the process.

Dr. Lindsey Thomas, a Minnesota medical examiner, explains the process:

> We typically start taking photographs the minute a body is brought in. We take them of the body clothed, because we want a shot of how the person looked when he came in. Plus, sometimes the clothing can offer clues of particular injuries. For example, if there is an abrasion around the neck that has a pattern to it, we can look at the clothing and say, "Oh, it's the ribbing of the neckline on this sweater or something—that caused the pattern."[73]

Critical information may be discovered during an autopsy. Here a medical examiner prepares to conduct an autopsy examination.

Thomas says that the body is then photographed without clothing. Just as the photographer at the crime scene did, Thomas will make certain there are several photographs that show any unusual or identifying marks or tattoos, and facial shots that can be shown to family members to verify identification. Then she will take close-up photographs of wounds or other injuries. "The idea," she says, "is that later a jury may need to look at these to see what I saw when I did the autopsy."[74]

What the Body Can Tell

Many times an autopsy reveals a much different result than expected. Perhaps what appears to be a homicide is not, or a death that does not seem suspicious turns out to be murder. In either case, photographs are crucial to showing the real cause of the death.

Thomas recalls a recent case in which the body of a woman was brought in, in what was not believed to be a homicide, but rather a heroin overdose. "She was a known drug user," she says, "and at the scene there was a syringe and a lot of alcohol bottles around. At first there was no reason to suspect it was anything *other* than a drug overdose."

But when she did the autopsy, Thomas realized that the crime scene had been staged. She says:

> We found that the hyoid bone in her neck had been broken. She had been strangled. It was interesting, because there were no marks on her, not even on her neck. And while she had a recent injection site in her arm—what we thought was from shooting heroin— the syringe was empty. Her boyfriend or husband or whatever had done it—he had most likely put water in it or something, and stuck it in her arm to make it look like she had been injecting heroin.[75]

All of this was photographed during the autopsy, so there was evidence that the death was unnatural and the evidence could be used in court. "Without the autopsy," Thomas says, "we would not have known."[76]

Thinking Like a Monster

One of the most unusual uses of photography after death occurs after the body has been embalmed for burial. For some reason, bruising is more evident then. Using an alternative light source, such as ultraviolet (UV) light and a special camera filter, an investigator or medical examiner can illuminate details on the body that would be invisible to the human eye.

This is especially useful when investigators may suspect that a child's death was not—as a parent may insist—due to a fall or illness, but the result of violence. Photographs of certain types or patterns of bruising under the skin can verify this—allowing police to begin an investigation of homicide. One photographer says he routinely visits mortuaries with a UV light and filter before the burial of a child when such abuse is suspected:

> I've seen this with infants and babies so many times. . . . It's like an hour before the funeral. What the bulk of them are—you can see where somebody hit them with a fist. There will be these little patches, two or three inches square. And you'll see these all over the face, the chest, the stomach. It's where they've been beaten to death. It'll show up, with the [special light].[77]

Forensic scientist Michael Calistro says that such photography requires a trained eye and an ability to visualize how that child could have been killed without leaving visible marks. He explains:

> Like if you have a little baby and the [UV] light shows two little circular bruises on the chest. And you turn the kid around and there are eight round bruises on the back. Experience helps—you've seen that before. It means the baby has been picked up and held hard and

The medical examiner is accompanied by an official photographer to document every step of the autopsy.

shaken. Unfortunately in this job, you've got to think like a monster to catch a monster.[78]

A Bite Mark

Sometimes photographs at an autopsy can lead to an even more specific discovery—the identity of the murderer. Many

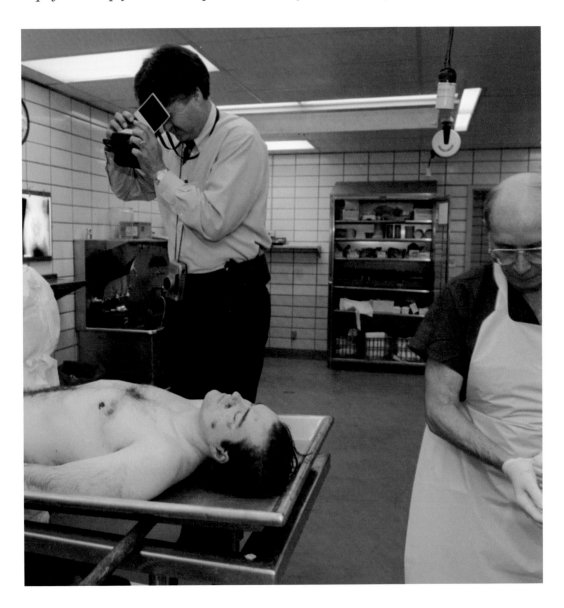

rapists and murderers bite their victims, and during an autopsy, the medical examiner will take detailed, close-up photographs of the bite mark. By comparing the mark to the teeth of a suspect, it is very possible to prove that person's guilt.

One of the most famous cases of bite mark identity was that of serial killer Ted Bundy, who is believed to have murdered between forty and fifty women (though some investigators say it could be far more) in Florida, Utah, Colorado, Oregon, and Washington. On January 15, 1978, after having escaped from jail, Bundy strangled and clubbed to death four young women at Florida State University. Police recovered no fingerprints at the scene, but one of the murdered women had a deep bite mark—presumably from her attacker.

The medical examiner photographed the bite mark, and later, when Bundy was arrested on suspicion of having committed the murders, detectives were able to force Bundy to submit to having an impression made of his teeth. His bite was unusual because it was very uneven, according to experts, and the impression was found to match up exactly with the photograph of the bite mark on the murder victim. It was on that evidence that Bundy was found guilty and later sentenced to death.

Identifying an Unknown Victim

Photographs also play a very important role in verifying the identification of an unknown victim. Medical examiners not only take photos of the victim's face (head-on and in profile), but they also take photos of distinguishing marks on the body, such as tattoos or scars. These photos are usually different from those taken by the crime scene photographer, which are limited to those marks visible without disturbing the position of the body at the scene. During an autopsy, clothes are removed so tattoos and other marks on the body that were not evident at the scene can be photographed.

Tattoos can be especially helpful in identifying a body that has been decomposing. As a body breaks down, the skin begins to slough, or slip off, as it deteriorates. Some marks on the skin that were obvious before death may not be when the body is in this condition. However, a tattoo goes under the top layer of skin to the dermis underneath. It can still be photographed and used to verify a victim's identity.

Medical examiners often utilize a different sort of imaging to try to identify a victim—X-rays. Created by high-energy radiation through film, an X-ray allows the examiner to see inside the body, down through the bones. If a person has an implant, such as a pacemaker or an artificial hip—those

What Tattoos Can Tell

In their book Dead Reckoning: The New Science of Catching Killers, *Michael Baden and Marion Roach explain the importance of documenting a body's tattoos—not only for identification, but for understanding what sort of person he or she was in life.*

Tats, or tacs, or ink, the cops call them. Reading ink is a valuable recognition and interpretation skill for the medical examiner. In the case of an unknown body it can unlock the identity: Some armed forces tattoos may even include name, rank, and serial number. A convict's tattoo, or joint tat, can be just as revealing and can tell me who he is and where he's been and what he's done. . . . For instance, a clock without hands means doing time, as do spider webs on elbows or shoulders. A happy face twinned with a crying face means play now, pay later. A man emblazoned with the face of a crying female means there is someone waiting on the outside. The Mexican Mafia, Aryan brotherhood, black guerrillas, Southerners, Northerners, all manners of groups have distinguishing inks.

Michael Baden and Marion Roach, *Dead Reckoning: The New Science of Catching Killers.* New York: Simon & Schuster, 2001, p. 31.

details can be crucial in verifying the person's identity. In many cases, medical implants have serial numbers, which may allow the examiner to trace them to the name of the doctor who performed the implant—and then to the name of the patient.

Another Use of X-Rays

In the case of a victim of a fire or explosion, or when the body has been extremely decomposed in water, for example, X-ray imagery can be even more vital as a means of identification. In such cases, a person's facial features are unrecognizable, and fingerprints are almost impossible to get. But teeth are more hardy. One of the most valuable methods of identification used by medical examiners is dental X-rays.

Minnesota medical examiner Michael McGee says that even when bodies are in fairly good shape, he has more success with dental X-rays than fingerprints:

> Unless you are a police officer, or are in the security business, or you've served in the armed services, or you have a criminal record, you haven't got fingerprints on file. So even if [investigators are] lucky enough to get a fingerprint from a body, running it through the [AFIS] database, [they will] never get a match, never find out who it belongs to.[79]

On the other hand, he says, most people have visited dentists. They have had teeth filled and had teeth X-rayed. And dentists routinely keep copies of patients' dental X-rays on file.

When the identity of the body is not certain, the medical examiner will take an X-ray image of the teeth, noting fillings as well as other work, such as crowns, false teeth, or evidence of root canal surgery. Once the body's teeth have been charted, they compare the chart to the dental records of any likely victim.

By the Numbers

8,000

Number of body bags ordered by New York City medical examiner's office yearly.

"The Most Important Thing of All"

The photographs and other images taken of the body in order to identify it are as important as those that can provide clues to the murderer. Medical examiners and others who take such photographs think of themselves as representatives of each body brought to them. One forensic technician says:

> I had a medical examiner say that he thinks of himself as standing for the dead. The victims can't speak any longer, but the evidence on their body can tell us a lot if we are willing to look hard enough. And sometimes, even if they are not successful in finding documentation [to arrest the murderer] they can at least provide the victim's identity. In some cases—especially for the families—that's the most important thing of all.[80]

CHAPTER 5

Photographing Crime as It Happens

The crime scene photographer and medical examiner take images after a crime has occurred. They hope the evidence and information they document will provide investigators with clues so that the criminals can be found. However, photographs and video come from other sources. These images are most intriguing, for many of them show the crime as it actually took place.

These images range in type and source—from security video taken by cameras in convenience stores and ATMs to police surveillance tapes. The images also come from witnesses to a crime who alertly take photos with a cell phone, and some are videos that are taken by criminals themselves, never suspecting the images might be used later to send them to prison.[81]

Security Video

Security tapes are the most widely used by investigators. These are taken by cameras mounted in places to capture images of trespassers, robbers, or vandals. "People don't notice them half the time," says Dave, a former police officer. "They're up high, mounted way above doorways or on the roofs outside buildings. They're at the ATM machine, and even in parking lots. You don't even realize how many places are taking your picture day and night."

But police are aware of them. In fact, one of the first things they do after a robbery or other crime occurs is to look for security cameras that might have caught the event on tape. "It sounds like a great system, lots of cameras catching criminals doing their bad deeds," says Dave. "But the truth is, and everyone will tell you this, is that the tapes are often very poor quality.

By the Numbers

80

Number of times the average American appears on video each day.

Store managers don't replace them often enough, and just keep taping over them, over and over. They're down to the last molecule of film, and results are lousy."[82]

Bill Hinz agrees wholeheartedly. "It's true—the result we get is pretty terrible a lot of the time," he says. "You want to tell these people, 'Hey, it's not expensive to use a new tape once in awhile.' They're probably saving about three bucks—big deal."

Hinz says another aspect of store video that frustrates investigators is that the cameras are often not aimed where they should be. "Unfortunately, most of these gas stations, convenience stores, whatever—they install their video systems so they are much more beneficial to the business owner than the police. They focus on the employee behind the counter so that the employee doesn't steal, instead of getting shots of who's going to walk in the door and rob the place—or worse."[83]

"What We Do Is, We Turn on the Lights"

But even with poor placement of the cameras and grainy quality of the tape, investigators can get a great deal of information from security tapes. This is due in large part to the work of the video analysis unit. These men and women can extract a great deal of information from tapes that are, to the average person, merely shadows and blurry shapes.

Clifford Johnson, a video analyst for the Minneapolis Police Department, says he uses what is a kind of simplistic metaphor for his job:

What we do is, we turn on the lights. If you walk into a room with no lights on, you can't see what's in there. Video analysis basically turns on the lights. We don't change anything—we don't alter the content of the tape at all. But when I say we turn on the lights, we may improve the contrast of the image, or enlarge part of the image, or add lighting so it's clearer, so investigators and later, juries, can do their work. We're just turning the lights on, so people can see.[84]

During a school shooting in Florida, security video shows a student pointing a gun at a teacher and student.

From Tape to Digital

Kimberly Meline, a video specialist with the Saint Paul Police Department, explains that when she receives a security video, her first step is to get it into a digital format. Once it is digital, she can work on enhancing the image. Meline explains the process:

> First I put the tape in the VCR, which feeds a cable that goes into my computer system. I use this computer to enhance, or improve, the video. That basically means cleaning it up, getting better clarity, enlarging parts of it that may be of interest to the investigators. So my computer system records the light levels and color levels that are coming by cable from the VCR, and it puts them in digital format.

At that point, she says, she can look at the image frame by frame. She says:

> See, normal video, when it goes through at thirty frames per second, you can't see individual frames— it's way too fast. What the computer allows me to do when I'm looking at each frame, is to pick out the best views of something—maybe a face, a gun, whatever. And a lot of time, what I do, is take that best view and make a still of it, like a photograph, so police can use it maybe to show around, to identify the person.[85]

An Unusual Tattoo

Meline says that it is surprising that, even with poor quality tape, the analyst can get a frame that shows a decent view of something that may help investigators.

"We had a case recently, where a convenience store was burglarized at night," she recalls. "No one was there at the time, so no witnesses. I couldn't get any facial images of the person, because he had a hoodie over his head. But he did have his sleeves rolled up, so I was able to see a tattoo."[86]

She says that the tattoo was important because even though she could not see details, it was in an unusual spot. "It was lower, down on the forearm, rather than the bicep—which is more common. Plus, it was a pretty unusual shape. So I gave the investigator a nice image of that."[87]

Although such an image is not enough to convict someone of a crime, it did help the detective narrow her search for suspects. "Actually, she came back a few weeks later and said it really helped," says Meline. "They'd been looking at one suspect, but had no real proof that it was him. But he had a tattoo like

Here a police officer monitors surveillance tape to identify a criminal. Video can often convict criminals.

that, in the same place, same shape. So it gave them a reason to step up their investigation of that guy. It was a nice case—they're currently in the process of prosecuting that one."[88]

Proving a Pornographer a Liar

Occasionally, analysts can enhance a single small detail that is so powerful it can send someone to prison for many years. That was the case in a pornography crime, in which a man was

"You Will Plead Guilty, Because It Was You"

Video analyst Clifford Johnson says some of the most interesting effects of crime video are on the families of the accused. Johnson recalls:

We had an example of that in Minneapolis not long ago. The defendant had pled not guilty right up until the trial. But right before the trial started, his family asked to see the surveillance video. They knew it existed—I don't know if they just wanted to see for themselves that it was him, or they didn't believe he had done the crime. But they viewed it before the trial in [the judge's] chambers.

And when they finished viewing it, they went right out to the defendant—their son—and said, "You *will* plead guilty, because it was you." When they saw that video—and we'd worked on it here in the lab—they basically said, no, we're not arguing. Admit the crime and take your punishment. There's a lot of times when that happens. They'll see photographic and video evidence and see themselves and realize, why am I arguing?

Clifford Johnson, telephone interview, December 9, 2007.

on trial for making and distributing pornography. He admitted that he had done it, but said that it was more than seven years ago. The statute of limitations for that crime was seven years—so one could not be prosecuted after that long.

But federal prosecutors had reason to believe the films were more recent. They sent them to the FBI's lab to see if technicians there could see something that would disprove the suspect's claim. A lab technician went through the film frame by frame to see if there was something that would prove the film was less than seven years old.

He painstakingly enlarged any frame that had material in the background and viewed it with a high-powered magnifier. He was able to find one shot with a bookshelf in the background, and under the magnifier, found a J.C. Penney catalog that was only five years old. That proved the man was lying, and because the statute of limitations had not run out, he was charged for the crime.

Help from Many Angles

Video analysts say that when a crime is committed, their search for helpful videotape usually goes beyond the office or business where the crime occurred. In fact, several nearby stores or offices—or even traffic cameras—may have captured an image that could help investigators solve the crime.

Dave, a retired police officer, recalls an armed robbery case at a downtown liquor store several years ago:

> There were three of these guys—two went in the store and one was in the car, keeping it running to keep it warm. This was in January, it was ten below or something —really cold. So the guy keeping the car running parks around the corner from the liquor store. He figured he'd be the smart guy—so there would be no video of the car from the liquor store—they had cameras outside in their parking lot and at the front door.

Dave says the plan did not work. He explains:

We went out after the robbery looking for nearby businesses with [video] systems, and found a chiropractor on the side street where the car was idling. The chiropractor had been broken into a couple months before, and installed a good system. And sure enough, we got a real good image of the car, a busted taillight, and a couple other things that made this car easy to spot.[89]

Restoring Damaged Tape

A lot of criminals try to avoid being recorded on tape by destroying the video camera or VCR system. Interestingly, however, that very act can sometimes provide investigators with excellent facial images. Clifford Johnson explains:

The thing is, when someone walks in the door of a gas station or a convenience store—something like that—they've already had their image recorded. They don't realize it, so that's good. What we end up with a lot of times is a great full-face of a guy who ripped the camera off the wall so it wouldn't photograph him. Then they unplug it or yank it off the wall, or rip the tape out of the housing, but it's too late by then. In fact, that image we recover will be better than anything we'd have gotten if they'd just left [the camera] there—very identifiable.[90]

Experts says that it is not terribly difficult to repair or restore damaged tape. Kimberly Meline says:

I do it all the time. I've had videos turned in to me where the suspect has yanked it out of the VCR, thinking they're erasing the tape. Or they'll smash the tape or the VCR, thinking it's destroyed. But usually it isn't. I've been known to sit here manually rewinding the tape—maybe splicing it and putting it back into a new plastic case. And most of the time, it works fine. Even tape that has gotten wet can almost always be salvaged.[91]

"We Do a Lot of Things in Here That No One Else Has Tried"

Some of the most challenging restorations are sent to the FBI's Video Enhancement Unit. These are tapes that local and state law enforcement labs are reluctant to touch, because they are so fragile. "Tapes arrive in the lab in every conceivable condition," reports forensic researcher David Fisher. "They have been burned and scratched and scraped and stretched and twisted and cut into pieces. They have been erased and flushed down toilets and retrieved from plane crashes and garbage dumps."[92]

Video technicians enhance the quality of a surveillance tape. Additional clarity of details may lead to arrest and conviction.

In many cases it would be a victory just to restore a frame or two on such a tape. This was the case when a military aircraft flew into a mountain and experts needed to know why. The pilots gave no indication that they were in trouble before the crash. Whether the tragedy was due to a sudden weather problem or even foul play of some sort, it was crucial to get answers.

In the nose of the plane was a video recorder that records the images seen by the pilots. However, the tape was in terrible condition. "The military came to us with some mangled tape that had been retrieved from the wreckage and asked if there was anything we could do with it," recalls a technician in the lab. "I didn't think there was. I mean, this stuff looked like strands of spaghetti. . . . It had kind of shriveled up in the fire."

Technicians tried flattening it by putting a wet cloth over it and ironing it. They were excited to see that the tape was not as badly damaged as they had first believed. "We were finally able to play it," says the technician. "I didn't know what I was looking at, but there were two military pilots working with us, and as soon as they saw this thing, they knew exactly what had happened. And basically, it turned out to be pilot error."[93]

Help from NASA

In some cases even when analysts work to enhance or restore a video, it does not provide enough information to catch a dangerous criminal. In a few instances, where time is a factor and the case is life-and-death, video analysts have enlisted the help of space scientists at NASA. This happened after the disappearance of eleven-year-old Carlie Brucia in Sarasota, Florida, in February 2004. She was walking home from a sleepover at a friend's house, and her route took her through the parking lot of a car wash.

Video from the car wash was disappointing. It showed a man in his twenties or thirties stopping the girl and leading her away. But the tape had a jerky quality that made it impossible to hone in on details that could help identify the man—and hopefully save the little girl.

Police sent the tape to NASA scientists, who had a special software program to deal with the jerkiness of the video. The program is typically used to compensate for that same wobbly quality—both vertically and horizontally—that appears in satellite images from space. Experts at NASA were able to use their software to extract details from the tape, such as tattoos on the man's arms and a particular kind of

NASA used special software to enhance a jerky videotape showing Carlie Brucia being abducted by a man in Florida.

18:21:41 02/01/2004

uniform shirt that he was wearing. They made stills of the images of the man and released them to the media. Within hours police had calls from people who recognized him. Though tragically it was too late to save the little girl, the man responsible was arrested and convicted.

An Odd Twist

Sometimes a case is solved by an odd twist—a fluke that a photograph is taken, and a fluke that it is viewed by just the right person. One of the strangest—and luckiest—of these cases began on Christmas Eve, 2001, when a baby named Jasmine

A Noncrime on Video

Sometimes security video can provide investigators with proof that a crime did not occur, thereby saving the police countless hours of wasted time. Kimberly Meline, a video analyst for the Saint Paul Police Department, recalls a case in which a young woman had reported a sexual assault.

She said that she had been assaulted behind a particular restaurant. But when we went to collect security video, we saw there was no camera in the back, where the assault was alleged to have taken place. But there was a dentist's office next door, with video. The investigator went and got that video—but it showed no assault. At the time she said she was being assaulted, we had clear images of her walking around the parking lot, talking on her cell phone. We don't know the motive in the false report—maybe she needed the attention. But the video showed there had been no assault, and that was good.

Kimberly Meline, personal interview, December 7, 2007, Saint Paul, MN.

Anderson was kidnapped from a bus station in Chicago. The woman who kidnapped the baby had offered to hold the child, who was fussing, while Jasmine's mother, Marcella, exchanged tickets at the counter. When she turned around, Marcella realized what had happened.

The kidnapper, Sheila Harris, took the baby back to a Chicago suburb where her own family lived. She had not seen them in some time and was able to pass the baby off as her own. Harris told her boyfriend (whom she had not seen for more than a year) that the child was his, and although he was surprised, he had no reason to doubt the story.

Meanwhile, police were stymied. The large bus station offered few clues. That close to Christmas there were thousands of people, and there was no way of checking that many fingerprints. In addition, as is the case with so many security cameras, those at the bus station were all trained on employees, so there was no video showing the kidnapping.

Pictures, and More Pictures

The break came for investigators because of two kinds of photographs. The first were those taken by the kidnapper's family. Sheila Harris's mother, delighted and proud that she had a new grandchild, took them by the dozen to be made into wallet-sized photos to send to her friends and relatives. Although Harris did not want pictures taken (for obvious reasons), the new grandmother took them anyway. "What do you mean?" she asked her daughter. "This is my granddaughter? I'm gonna take lots of pictures!"[94]

At the same time, the police released photos of the missing child to the media. Every station throughout the country broadcast pictures of little Jasmine Anderson. Every newspaper showed the baby, too. And when Harris's mother got her own photos developed, she realized who the baby really was.

She took her photographs and went to the police, who were then able to return Jasmine to her family. Says one police officer who worked on the case, "The evidence here came from pictures—the ones the real mother gave the media and the ones the kidnapper's family took at Christmas."[95]

Pictures of the Criminal, by the Criminal

Video analysts say they are always amazed at the circumstances that produce results in their labs. "In some cases, it's the criminal him- or herself that is responsible for the video," says Kimberly Meline.

She gives an example of young gang members who record themselves on their cell phones:

> We had a case of this one guy, who had his friend video him on his phone—he was spouting off, showing his gang signs, showing his colors, his guns. He was making all kinds of threats, too—against his ex-girlfriend, against police officers, whatever. Just bravado, showing off for one another, I think.
>
> Anyway, very soon after that recording was made, he went and robbed a convenience store—and in the process, he dropped his phone. The investigator brought the phone to me, not knowing whether there was anything helpful on it. And I was able to give the detective some nice images of the man, his threats, and everything else—good enough to arrest and prosecute him for that robbery.[96]

"It's Not Just About the Technology"

The use of photography to solve crimes comes in a variety of forms—from the forensics unit that documents the crime scene to the citizen who takes a picture of a crime in progress. Experts believe that the quality and capacity of photography is improving, and that can only be a good thing for fighting crime.

They cite security video as a good example. Fifteen years ago, it was rare for a business to include photography as part of a security system. The price was far higher than today, says Kimberly Meline, and that kept many people from investing in it. "They probably had no idea how important video could be. Now, the price is so low, places can get a great deal of [video] coverage for their business. The quality is far better than in years past. And now it's rare to find a place without a system. And it really pays off—we see evidence of it every day."[97]

Experts say that such advances are occurring in the field, too. With the improvement in digital photography and new ideas in processing crime scenes—such as more use of alternate light sources—forensic units will be able to get more detail from crime scenes. "But the nice thing is, it's not just about the technology," says forensic photographer Steve Banning. "It's also about creativity by those in the field, figuring out ways to make a [crime] scene come to life. It's making things that were invisible—or barely visible—easy enough to see that an inexperienced eye of someone on the jury will be able to understand what they're looking at."[98]

By the Numbers

11

Average number of hours needed to retrieve deleted video from cell phone.

Notes

Introduction: A Thousand Heartbreaking Words

1. Amy, telephone interview, November 6, 2007.

2. Quoted in Connie Fletcher, *Every Contact Leaves a Trace*. New York: St. Martin's, 2006, p. 61.

3. Steve Banning, personal interview, November 9, 2004, Saint Paul, MN.

4. Name withheld, personal interview, November 16, 2007, Richfield, MN.

5. Amy, interview.

Chapter One: A Vital Responsibility

6. Amy, interview.

7. Amy, interview.

8. Quoted in Fletcher, *Every Contact Leaves a Trace*, p. 7.

9. Dencell, telephone interview, November 14, 2007.

10. Dencell, interview.

11. Dencell, interview.

12. Quoted in Fletcher, *Every Contact Leaves a Trace*, p. 9.

13. Quoted in Fletcher, *Every Contact Leaves a Trace*, p. 9.

14. Hinz, personal interview, October 30, 2007, Minneapolis, MN.

15. Dave, telephone interview, November 30, 2007.

16. Hinz, interview.

17. Dan DeLeo, "Sampson Jurors View Graphic Murder-Scene Photography," *Quincy* (MA) *Patriot Ledger*, November 14, 2003, p. 9.

18. Quoted in DeLeo, "Sampson Jurors," p. 9.

19. Quoted in Fletcher, *Every Contact Leaves a Trace*, p. 321.

20. Michael Baden and Marion Roach, *Dead Reckoning: The New Science of Catching Killers*. New York: Simon & Schuster, 2001, p. 150.

21. Baden and Roach, *Dead Reckoning*, pp. 46–47.

Chapter Two: At the Scene of the Crime

22. David Fisher, *Hard Evidence: How Detectives Inside the FBI's Sci-Crime Lab Have Helped Solve America's Toughest Cases*. New York: Simon & Schuster, 1995, p. 266.

23. Dencell, interview.

24. Hinz, interview.

25. Quoted in Fletcher, *Every Contact Leaves a Trace*, p. 32.

26. Steve Banning, personal interview, November 21, 2007, Anoka, MN.

27. Dencell, interview.

28. N.E. Genge, *The Forensic Casebook*. New York: Ballantine, 2002, p. 223.

29. Hinz, interview.

30. Michael Calistro, personal interview, November 26, 2007, Minneapolis, MN.

31. Banning, interview.

32. Banning, interview.

33. Hinz, interview.

34. Quoted in Fletcher, *Every Contact Leaves a Trace*, p. 32.

35. Sean McKenna, personal interview, September 30, 2004, Minneapolis, MN.

36. Banning, interview.

37. Banning, interview.

38. Banning, interview.

39. Dencell, interview.

40. Dencell, interview.

41. Dencell, interview.

42. Banning, interview.

43. Amy, interview.

44. Hinz, interview.

45. Hinz, interview.

46. Banning, interview.

Chapter Three: All in the Details

47. Quoted in Genge, *The Forensic Casebook*, p. 30.

48. Amy, interview.

49. Banning, interview.

50. Dencell, interview.

51. Calistro, interview.

52. Amy, interview.

53. David Peterson, personal interview, April 20, 2005, Saint Paul, MN.

54. Hinz, interview.

55. Banning, interview.

56. Banning, interview.

57. Jarrett Hallcox and Amy Welch, *Bodies We've Buried: Inside the National Forensic Academy, the World's Top CSI Training School*. New York: Berkley, 2006, p. 39.

58. Quoted in Fletcher, *Every Contact Leaves a Trace*, p. 145.

59. Quoted in Fletcher, *Every Contact Leaves a Trace*, pp. 139–40.

60. Dencell, interview.

61. Calistro, interview.

Chapter Four: The Body as a Crime Scene

62. Amy, interview.

63. Quoted in Fletcher, *Every Contact Leaves a Trace*, p. 39.

64. Quoted in Fletcher, *Every Contact Leaves a Trace*, p. 33.

65. Banning, interview.

66. Banning, interview.

67. Quoted in Fletcher, *Every Contact Leaves a Trace*, p. 37.

68. Amy, interview.

69. Quoted in Fisher, *Hard Evidence*, p. 158.

70. Quoted in Fisher, *Hard Evidence*, p. 158.

71. Dencell, interview.

72. Banning, interview.

73. Lindsey Thomas, personal interview, December 4, 2007, Minneapolis, MN.

74. Thomas, interview.

75. Thomas, interview.

76. Thomas, interview.

77. Quoted in Fletcher, *Hard Evidence*, p. 191.

78. Calistro, interview.

79. Michael McGee, personal interview, December 8, 2004, Saint Paul, MN.

80. Amy, interview.

Chapter 5: Photographing Crime as It Happens

81. Dave, interview.

82. Dave, interview.

83. Hinz, interview.

84. Clifford Johnson, telephone interview, December 9, 2007.

85. Kimberly Meline, personal interview, December 7, 2007, Saint Paul, MN.

86. Meline, interview.

87. Meline, interview.

88. Meline, interview.

89. Dave, interview.

90. Johnson, interview.

91. Meline, interview.

92. Fisher, *Hard Evidence*, p. 279.

93. Quoted in Fisher, *Hard Evidence*, p. 280.

94. Quoted in Fletcher, *Every Contact Leaves a Trace*, p. 58.

95. Quoted in Fletcher, *Every Contact Leaves a Trace*, p. 58.

96. Meline, interview.

97. Meline, interview.

98. Banning, interview.

Glossary

AFIS: The Automatic Fingerprint Identification System, a computer system that can help investigators compare a fingerprint to millions of other prints that have been entered into the system.

autopsy: An examination of a dead body by a medical examiner.

blood spatter: Patterns of blood drops that have fallen or sprayed from the victim. These are photographed and evaluated to provide clues to the attack.

enhance: To make better; improve the quality of.

impression: A three-dimensional mark that is made by a shoe, a tire, or a fingerprint in something soft.

latent print: A fingerprint that is invisible.

lifting: The act of actually removing a fingerprint or footprint using powders or chemicals and then placing the image on an evidence card using tape. Before prints are lifted, they must be photographed.

Luminol: A combination of chemicals that can make bloodstains fluoresce, or glow.

shutter: The mechanical part of a camera that opens and closes the lens opening to expose the film to light.

tripod: A three-legged stand on which a camera can be mounted to keep it steady.

For More Information

Books

Paul Dowling, *The Official Forensic Files Casebook*. New York: iBooks, 2004. Very readable account of the solving of various crimes. Good explanation of surveillance video and the value of photography.

Henry C. Lee, *Cracking Cases: The Science of Solving Crimes*. Amherst, NY: Prometheus, 2002. Excellent colorful crime scene photos from a number of famous cases, showing the use of scale by the photographer.

Richard Platt, *Crime Scene: The Ultimate Guide to Forensic Science*. New York: DK, 2003. Very readable, with riveting photographs detailing the steps in investigating various crimes.

Edward M. Robinson, *Crime Scene Photography*. London: Academic, 2007. Though this is very difficult reading, the book can provide a great deal of information for a motivated reader. Good examples of various technical aspects of photography, with plenty of photos.

Periodicals

Janet Rausa Fuller, "Clues Came Together for 'Grandma' Who Alerted Cops," *Chicago Sun-Times*, December 29, 2001.

Frank Roylance, "NASA Scientists Help Clarify Clues in Fla. Missing Girl Case," *Baltimore Sun*, February 5, 2004.

Web Sites

Crime Library: Criminal Minds and Methods (www.crimelibrary.com/criminal_mind/forensics/crimescene/3.html). This site links basics of photography with criminal cases that have hinged on good photographic documentation.

Crime Scene Investigation (www.crime-scene-investigator.net/index.html). This site has links to dozens of articles about various aspects of crime scene photography, including use of flash, alternative light sources, photographing bruises, and the use of video.

Crime Scene Photography (www.geocities.com/cfpdlab/csphoto.html). This is an extremely helpful Web site, with links to various papers on both well-known and novel approaches to photography by law enforcement. There are interesting articles on photography in cases of domestic violence, blood spatter, as well as the use of digital photography. There are no visuals, but the reading material is well done.

Index

Picture Credits

Cover Photos: Image copyright JustASC, 2008. Used under license from Shutterstock.com; Image copyright emin kuliyev, 2008. Used under license from Shutterstock.com

AP Images, 10, 17, 23, 25, 30, 33, 35, 39, 56

© Bettmann/Corbis, 14

Anthony Bolante/Reuters/Landov, 9

Frank H. Conlon/Getty Images, 21

Michael Donne/Photo Researchers, Inc., 45, 61

© Najlah Feanny/Corbis, 51

Mauro Fermariello/Photo Researchers, Inc., 67

Getty Images News/Getty Images, 85

Spencer Grant/Photo Researchers, Inc., 48

© John Griffin/The Image Works, 79

Ed Hille/MCT/Landov, 29

© Mikael Karlsson/Alamy, 62, 65

Abbas Momani/AFP/Getty Images, 83

© John Nakata/Corbis, 53

© Reuters/Corbis, 77

© Shepard Sherbell/Corbis Saba, 70

About the Author

Gail B. Stewart is the author of more than 200 books for young people. She is married and has three sons. She is a staunch fan of the Minnesota Twins and Gustavus Adolphus College men's soccer.